Fly Fishing For Kamloops Trout

Ray Gould

AuthorHouse™
1663 Liberty Drive
Bloomington, IN 47403
www.authorhouse.com
Phone: 1-800-839-8640

©2010 Ray Gould. All rights reserved.

No part of this book may be reproduced, stored in a retrieval system, or transmitted by any means without the written permission of the author.

First published by AuthorHouse   8/12/2010

ISBN: 978-1-4520-5456-8 (sc)

Library of Congress Control Number: 2010911403

Printed in the United States of America
Bloomington, Indiana

This book is printed on acid-free paper.

Dedication

This book is dedicated to the Fresh Water Fishing Society of BC and the wonderful rainbow trout often known as Kamloops trout. Few words can adequately describe the fantastic nature of that trout, but some that come to mind are strong, powerful, silvery, fighting, leaping, and coming readily to the fly.

British Columbia has excelled at managing their trout fishery for a long time. The BC government has recently created a partnership and placed the stocking of hatchery trout and the operation of five hatcheries in the hands of a nonprofit organization known as The Fresh Water Fishing Society of BC. Their nine-million-fish stocking program covers some one thousand lakes and streams and ensures there will be rainbow, steelhead, cutthroat, kokanee, and eastern brook trout for all to enjoy. They also provide conservation services for ecosystems and species at risk.

The vision of the Fresh Water Fishing Society is to be "The best freshwater fishery in North America," and indeed they are!

Acknowledgments

It has been wonderful having a really fine expert such as my daughter, LeaAnn Gould, to help me out every time a difficult situation arose regarding how to use the computer. Certainly the personal computer can do much more than I'll ever learn, but to LeaAnn it's just "no problem, Dad." Besides that, it has been good for me to learn new things. It's been a wonder watching how quickly a young, bright mind works.

A big thanks is due to Wilbur Watson, my longtime fishing partner, a fly pattern inventor and a very skilled fly fisher who reviewed of a previous book of mine. He willingly undertook the somewhat daunting task of writing the introduction for this book and editing it as well. You'll find his insights to be a refreshing new look at what fly fishing is all about and how it catches all who try it in its magnetism and camaraderie.

Authorhouse.com shows their fine skills in shaping the manuscript to make it attractive and presentable. Their staff has been more than helpful in designing the book and preparing the layout.

To the British Columbia's Department of Ministry of Labour and Citizen's Services, I owe a special thanks for patiently reviewing my requests for using copyrighted material. Their Intellectual Property Program's copyright officer, Ilona Ugro, was especially helpful in providing that permission. This was key to doing the research and collecting data necessary to support this book.

Sean Simmons, publisher of the *Angler's Atlas*, was likewise helpful in providing permission to use a few of their published maps. They too are an excellent source of information for anglers.

Another fine bit of assistance came by way of Dave Prentice, CEO of the Interactive Broadcasting Corporation, by providing permission to use some of their data and contour maps shown through their excellent publication called *BC Adventures*.

A salute must be included for Leo Parr, a longtime friend and associate who worked with me at Scott Paper Company for many years. He was as an extremely talented machinist and an artist as well. Leo created all the cartoons shown in the article "The Saga of The Leaky Tiki." What a marvelously multitalented man he was!

I simply cannot thank my group of fly fishing friends enough for all of the wonderful trips we've had together over the past fifty years in exploring the wilds of British Columbia while pursuing the wily Kamloops trout. So here's a salute to: Bob Barr, Perry Barth, Bill Booth, Bob Burdick, Jack Byrd, Ben Cain, Theron Chamberlain, Hugh Clark, Roy Dunbar, Jim Gauntt, Earl Gutschmidt, Dick Hankinson, Russ Hardy, Dick Hedges, Tom Hodgson, Bill Johnston, Roger Hutchings, Harry Kimball, Bob Lindemeyer, John Narver, Steve Raymond, Hal Rowe, Jarrett Schulz, Mike Shellito, Maury Skeith, Jim Swift, John Tibbs, Bill Vincent, Wil Watson, Marv Young, and Terry Zeitner. There's a vast amount of things to be learned from fly fishing friends, including fly tying, casting, cooking, and enjoying nature as well. One of the things that happens to most all fly fishers is an increase in their appreciation of the outdoors and the necessity to protect and preserve the environment. Many have honed their skills in photography, bird watching, and the identification of the bountiful wildflowers of the area. It all adds up to memorable times! Thanks too to Belle Marie Rightmire and Gordon Rightmire for their help in gathering data regarding Janice Lake.

One of the things I've learned about having a cabin in British Columbia is how wonderful it is to have neighbors such as Norm and Silke Cloutier, Mike and Shiley Ann Shellito and Bob Herrmann. They are simply the best friends one could want.

Contents

Introduction	xi

Chapter 1
The Mysterious Kamloops Trout	1
Triploids	3
Hatcheries	5

Chapter 2
Special Information Can Give You an Edge	7
Fish Stocking Density in Twenty-six of the Best Lakes in BC	9
Last Five Years of Fish Planting for Twenty-six of the Best Lakes	10
Fish Finders and Depth Sounders	11
Fly Rods and Reels	13
Fishing in the Evening	13
Successful Fishing Techniques	14
The Long-handled Net	15
Understanding What It Means When a Lake "Turns Over"	16

Chapter 3
26 of the Best Lakes in British Columbia	18
Badger Lake	19
Ballon Lake	21
Blue Lake	23
Calling Lake	25
Community Lake	27
Corbett Lake	29
Dardanelles Lake	31
Dragon Lake	33
Eliguk Lake	35
Fawn Lake	37
Glimpse Lake	39
Hatheume Lake	44
HiHium Lake	46
Big OK (Island) Lake	48
Janice Lake	51
Lac Le Jeune	53
Lundbom Lake	55
Marquart Lake	57

Minnie Lake	59
Peterhope Lake	61
Plateau Lake	63
Roche Lake	65
Stoney Lake	68
Stump Lake	70
Sullivan Lake (also known as Knouff Lake)	72
Tunkwa Lake	74

CHAPTER 4
Must-Have Flies — 76

My Three Favorite Flies — 76

Must-have Fly Patterns — 77

DRY FLIES — 78

Elk Hair Caddis Fly	78
Tom Thumb, Standard	79
Tom Thumb Green Body	80
Adams	81
Royal Wulff	82
Mosquito	83
Red Humpy	84
Yellow Humpy	85
Black Ant	86
Brown Sedge	87

WET FLIES — 88

Black O'Lindsay	88
Grizzly King	89
Self Carey	90
Black Carey	91
Pink Carey	92
Peacock Carey	93
Green Carey	94
Red Carey	95
Watson's Anomaly	96
Butt Ugly	97
Shrimp	98
Black Wooly Bugger	99
Black Marabou Leech	100
Dr. Spratley	101
Split Wing Spratley	102
Green Spratley	103
Thuya Spratley	104
Split Wing Thuya	105
Citation Spratley	106
Damsel	107
Liquid Lace Damsel	108

Nyerges	109
Sparkle Back Nyerges	110
Mylar Nyerges	111
Black Dragonfly Nymph	112
Green Dragon Fly Nymph	113
Olive Willie	114
Blood Worm	115
Glimpse Black Leech	116
Byrd's Black Magic	117
Brown Wooly Bugger	118
Jansen	119
Spruce Fly	120
Spruce Fly Nymph	121
Water Cricket	122
Royal Coachman Bucktail	123
Montana Nymph	124
Gils Monster	125
Pheasant Tail Nymph	126
Hares Ear	127
Water Boatman	128
CHIRONOMIDS	129
Ice Cream Cone with Wire Rib	129
Green Body Chironomid	130
Chromie	131
Big Head Chromie	132
Red Chironomid	133
Ice Cream Cone with Red Rib	134
Mike's gray chironomid	135

CHAPTER 5
Fly Hook Comparison Chart	136

CHAPTER 6
Boat Choices	138
Boats	138
Inflatables	140
Fold Boats	141
The Saga of the *Leaky Tiki*	144
The Problems Illustrated	144
Some Wonderful Solutions	145

CHAPTER 7
Cooking Trout	146
Barbequing the Kamloops Trout	146
Smoking Kamloops Trout	147

    Directions   147

    Trout Pâté (Source: Wil Watson)   147

Chapter 8
Discovering Nature   148

    The Birds of British Columbia   154

    Mushrooms   157

Chapter 9
Recommendations: Choosing the Right Place   158

    A list of especially worthy lakes to visit in British Columbia.   160

Chapter 10
When All Else Fails   161

Map Resources   163

Bibliography   164

Introduction

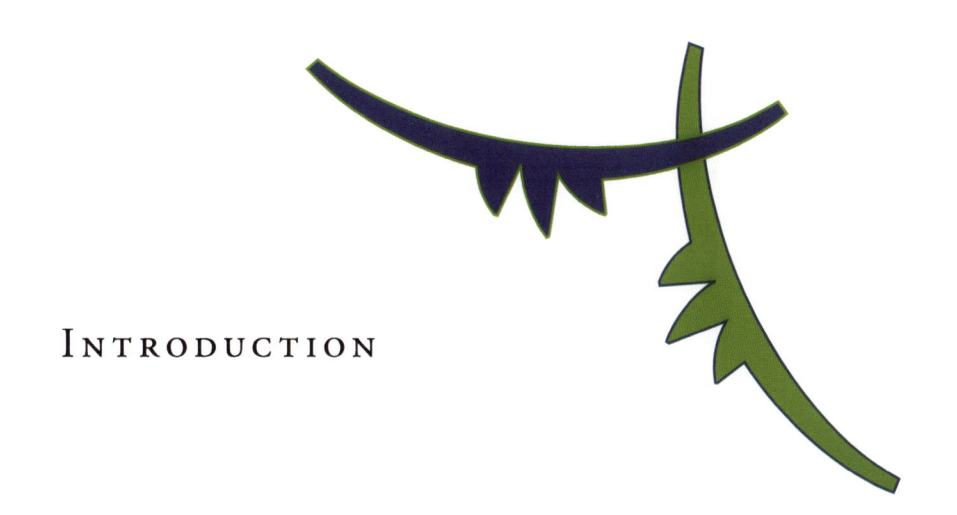

A QUICK REVIEW OF THE table of contents of this book, *Fly Fishing for Kamloops,* can provide only a hint of the depth and considerable value of what lies inside. However, with a full reading of the illustrative and comprehensive material in its pages, you may well reasonably hope to become a more knowledgeable, skillful, and successful angler. At the same time, you can experience the simple pleasure of obtaining an increased understanding of the history and nature of your prey.

This book presents the careful assembly of practical and useful information resulting from Ray Gould's fifty years of in-depth research, study, and last but not least, experience in virtually all of the major nuances of Kamloops trout fishing. Here you have an opportunity, as described in the author's own words, to get an edge by learning a great deal regarding the critical issues of "what, where, and how" in creating a memorable Kamloops trout fishing experience for yourself. While emphasis is clearly on fly fishing for Kamloops trout in British Columbia, the reader will find considerable information applicable to other trout fishing situations and environments as well.

Ray has, since the beginning of his fifty-year journey:

1. Become a skilled fly tyer and instructor affiliated with both the Northwest Fly Anglers Club (having served as president) and the Olympic Fly Fishers Club of Edmonds, Washington. Ray has tied many hundreds of Canadian trout flies in classical patterns and in more than a few of his own invention, which have proven to be highly successful. If you are not yet a fly tier, after reading this material you will probably find good reason to become one. Catching and fighting a Kamloops trout on your own secret fly is a glorious experience.

2. Drawing upon his study, engineering experience, and imagination, mastered the art of building Tonkin Cane (bamboo) fly rods. He became, and is currently, well-known in fly fishing circles as the guy to go to for evaluation or repair of existing bamboo rods and also as the builder and marketer of custom-made, new products. In this field Ray has written and successfully published two books. The first is *Constructing Cane Rods—Secrets of the Bamboo Fly Rod,* which is an informative book for any

angler with an interest in the history and mystique of bamboo rods in general and their construction and repair in particular.

3. His second book, *Cane Rods—Tips and Tapers,* is a more technical publication of particular value to those actually are involved in or interested in the exacting business of bamboo rod building or repair.

4. Additionally, Ray's devotion to fly fishing has extended well beyond the art of catching fish "for today's creel." He has been active in working with the members of The Fresh Water Fishing Society of BC and the staff of the British Columbia Fish and Wildlife in the critical areas of fish conservation and fish propagation management. This involvement has included collecting and providing the fisheries department with comprehensive logs of catch records and related data—all of which are designed to encourage the preservation and protection of the unique fishing opportunities in British Columbia.

To touch upon just a few of the several varied and useful topics addressed in this book, the very first chapter, "The Kamloops Trout," will introduce you to the origin and nature of this magnificent fish. In addition, the related information describing the advent and impact of the triploid process explains a subject unfamiliar to many. In "Must Have Flies," the descriptive material and colorful photos provide an excellent guide to readily help the angler make knowledgeable selections and avoid wasteful and ineffective purchases of the wrong stuff. A similar case can be made for "Twenty-six of the Best Lakes." In British Columbia one will find a huge number of lakes from which to choose. Such a broad range can be somewhat overwhelming, with an uninformed choice possibly disappointing. You will find considerable help here.

Also not to be missed is "Cooking the Trout." His suggestions for cooking, smoking, and creating trout pâté provide a great starting point for these rewarding activities. You may notice in this book certain other incidents, antics, and accounts that, although true, can best be described as entertaining.

Finally, from all these efforts and experiences, Ray has become not only a knowledgeable and skillful fly fisherman but a person who has achieved high levels of recognition as an outstanding craftsman, teacher, and conservationist as well. In this book he shares much of what he has learned and accomplished.

It has been my pleasure to have frequently fished alongside Ray ever since that first trip those fifty long years ago, and to have observed his constant growth as an angler and teacher and acknowledged leader in the game. I feel fortunate to have had such an opportunity.

Wilbur Watson

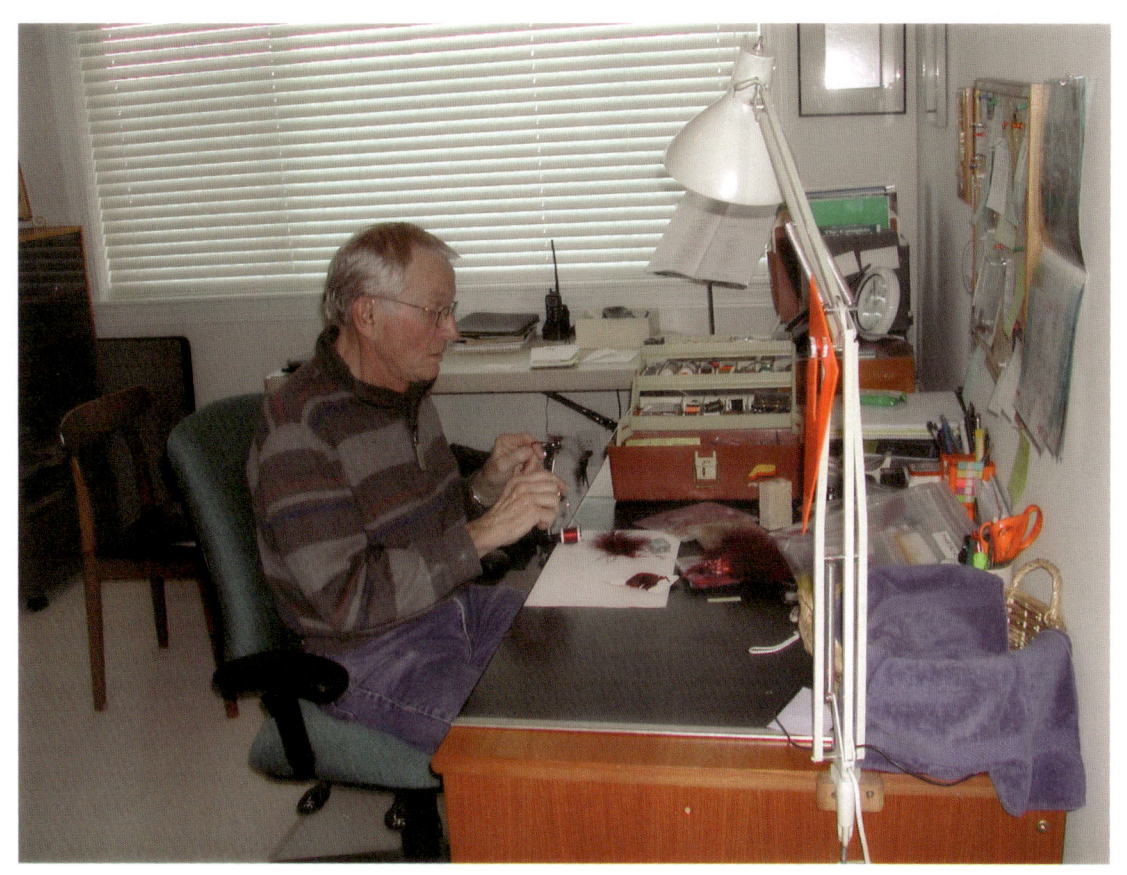

Wil at his fly tying desk

Chapter 1

The Mysterious Kamloops Trout

It all began some twelve thousand years ago. Huge glaciers covered most of the interior of British Columbia and what is now known as Washington State. When the glaciers melted, a vast lake covered the region, and it formed many lakes as it drained through the Columbia River system. It was during this time that rainbow trout developed and came to British Columbia.

Efforts to scientifically identify these trout have been undertaken several times especially since the early 1900s, when tales of these mighty fish began to spread among anglers. Fishing in the lakes of British Columbia produced trout of magnificent size, strength, and power. Many trout of ten to twenty pounds were taken, and really big fish, such as the fifty-three-pound fish from Jewel Lake, caused awe amongst anglers. Even today Kamloops trout of ten to fifteen pounds are occasionally taken.

But what were these fish? Were they really rainbows or were they another species? When Fort Kamloops was established in 1812, most of the small lakes were barren and only the larger lakes had resident fish. Yet tales of monster fish began to emerge over the next eighty years. Because of this, in 1892, a Dr. Jordan of Stanford University received samples for identification. He believed that these fish were different from rainbow trout and were named *Salmo Kamloops*, or Kamloops trout, as opposed to *Salmo gairdneri* for rainbow trout. Thus the name of the fish began. But the story does not end there. Further tests showed that the Kamloops strain was only different because of its environment and was genetically the same as the rainbow. So the classification of *Salmo Kamloops* was removed, and it is now known as *Oncorhychus mykiss*.

Therefore, there is indeed a Kamloops trout that is different in its fighting ability and characteristics because of its environment but is in fact genetically the same as the rainbow trout, the Gerrard trout of the Kootenays, the Blackwater trout of the Caribou, and the mighty steelhead trout.

Kamloops trout are basically insect eaters. Because of this fact, the trout readily take the fly—to the delight of fly fishers. Yet the Gerrard strain of Kootenay Lake are piscivores (fish eaters) and grow to be very large (they feed on Kokanee fry), as do the trout in Adams and Shuswap lakes. Another well-known strain is the famous Thompson River steelhead trout, famous for its size and strength.

The Freshwater Fishing Society of BC uses eight strains of rainbow trout. Three are based on wild populations (Pennask, Tzenzaicut, and Blackwater), three are native strains (dragon, premier, and Tunkwa), one is a wild population strain (Gerrard), and one is a domesticated strain (Fraser Valley). Each of these strains has particular characteristics and is then planted in suitable places for that fish.

Some interesting facts about Kamloops trout include the following:

- Trout usually spawn in their third or fourth year, although the fish-eating strains delay maturity until perhaps the fifth year.

- Trout eggs hatch into alevins in four to seven weeks depending on water temperature and become free swimming fry during the summer. Spawning stream water flows, temperature, and water levels are critical to good production. Many interior British Columbia lakes suffered from poor spawning stream production during low water, such as the years of 2003–2005.

- An adult rainbow can live as long as ten to eleven years. They spawn and return to the lake rather than dying, as do salmon.

- Kamloops trout use their senses of sight, smell, and hearing to survive. They have monocular vision in a large radius to the sides, back, and above, but they also have binocular vision in a small cone of vision toward the front.

It's every fly fisher's dream to tangle with one of these powerful fish. Lakes in British Columbia that contain the really big ones are often rather closely held secrets, though bragging sometimes lets the cat out of the bag. However, with the advent in recent years of triploid trout, quite a few lakes are turning out really big fish. Read on in this book, and you'll see the research and recommendations as to where big fish can be found.

But that's only part of the story. To be successful one can certainly benefit from the many techniques and tips offered throughout this book.

TRIPLOIDS

While this is an odd word, many fly fishers understand that "Triploid" means "big fish." Anglers often want to know where to go to catch a really big Kamloops trout. This chapter provides information to steer the fly fisher to the right spot.

So just exactly what is a triploid? A triploid is a genetically altered fish. It is sterile and does not reproduce but rather expends all of its energy toward rapid growth. These fish are specially reared and planted in many of the lakes in British Columbia, where they are avidly sought. The word "triploid" is actually a variation of the word "ploid," which refers to the number of chromosomes in a cell. "Haploid" means one chromosome, "diploid" means two chromosomes (what ordinary fish cells have), and "triploid" means three chromosomes.

Scientists have discovered they can create a triploid by treating the eggs with warm water temperature shortly after fertilization. Another method used is to place the eggs in a pressure vessel. What happens is that the fish end up with three chromosomes (triploid) instead of the normal two (diploid). This makes the fish sterile, which means they have to be reared and planted. The triploid fish have fewer but larger cells. Tests show that triploids have the same critical swimming speed, a measure of aerobic capacity, and the same stress response as diploids.

One question often asked is, "Are these triploids the same as the famous Donaldson trout reared by Professor Lauren Donaldson of the University Of Washington?" The answer is no. Donaldson trout originally came from Packwood Lake on Mount Rainier and were crossed with steelhead. They were selectively bred and given better nutrition so that they too grew very fast.

In the Thompson-Nicola area alone, over 130 lakes were planted with triploids (2007 data), and some are included in the 26 best lakes shown in this book. Please note that many of these lakes were also planted with triploids in prior years as well, and that some of the plants were fingerlings while others were yearlings. Among the better known lakes planted with triploids in 2005–2009 were those shown in the following chart: note that this chart shows only the triploid rainbows, although triploid brook trout, triploid kokanee, and diploid trout are also planted.

Rainbow Triploid Only Stocking in Some BC Lakes

(does not include diploids, brookies, or kokanees)

Lake	2005	2006	2007	2008	2009
Badger	1,277	-----	-----	-----	-----
Ballon	1,500	1,500	1,500	1,500	1,500
Bose	5,000	5,000	5,000	5,000	5,000
Blue	1,000	3,000	2,000	2,000	2,000
Community	1,000	1,000	1,000	1,000	1,000
Dardenelles	2,000	2,000	2,000	2,000	2,000
Dewar	1,000	6,000	5,331	11,000	-----
Dragon	10,033	10,000	10,261	10,079	10,050
Dugan	-----	20,000	20,000	20,000	20,000
Edith	5,500	9,000	9,000	8,000	4,500
Ernest	1,500	1,500	1,500	1,500	1,500
Fir	5,000	5,000	5,000	5,000	5,000
Fire	2,000	2,000	2,000	2,000	2,000
Forest	20,000	20,000	20,000	20,000	20,000
Frisken	8,000	8,000	8,000	8,000	8,000
Hammer	10,000	-----	10,000	10,000	10,000
Harmon	6,000	6,000	6,000	6,000	6,000
Hatheume	3,500	3,500	3,500	3,500	2,000
Hidden	15,000	15,000	15,000	15,000	15,000
Island (Big OK)	3,000	2,000	2,000	2,000	3,000
Jacko	3,500	3,500	3,500	3,500	3,032
Jimmy	1,500	1,500	1,500	1,500	1.500
Logan	3,500	3,500	3,500	3,500	1,000
Lodgepole	-----	-----	-----	-----	3,000
Lundbom	6,000	6,000	6,000	14,000	9,013
Lynn	2,000	2,000	2,556	2,520	2,548
Marquardt	4,000	4,000	4,500	4,500	-----
McConnell	5,000	5,000	5,000	5,000	5,000
Monte	20,000	10,000	20,000	20,000	15,000
Pass	2,000	2,000	3,000	2,000	4,000
Peter Hope	-----	-----	-----	12,000	12,045
Pinantan	4,000	4,000	4,000	4,000	-----
Roche	7,500	17,500	7,500	7,496	7,500
Red	9,000	13,242	11,763	9,309	9,000
Ross Moore	1,500	1,500	1,500	1,500	3,500
Silence	5,000	5,000	5,000	5,000	5,000
Sheridan	114,005	124,999	144,736	137,138	125,050
Stump	46,100	40,000	40,000	125,000	78,834
Tunkwa	------	15,000	15,000	20,000	25,049

Sue Gould with a dandy

HATCHERIES

There are five hatcheries in British Columbia operated by the Fresh Water Fishing Society of BC. Together these hatcheries stock some one thousand lakes and streams in British Columbia with more than six million trout, char, and kokanee annually.

The Vancouver Island Trout Hatchery is located at Duncan and raises rainbows, coastal cutthroat, and steelhead. This hatchery stocks about 150 lakes and streams on Vancouver Island and the surrounding islands. Their operating hours are Monday through Friday, 8:30 AM to 4:00 PM. There is a freshwater ecocenter adjacent to the hatchery that opens after April 1. It is an interpretive facility displaying fisheries management programs, fisheries habitat protection, and conservation efforts. It is heavily visited, so it is best to call ahead to check on their operating hours: 250-746-6722.

The **Clearwater Hatchery** is located in the town of Clearwater. Although originally built for producing salmon, it has been converted to use for rearing trout and kokanee. This hatchery stocks over 330 lakes annually with over 3 million rainbow trout (several strains), brook trout, and kokanee trout. It provides fish for most of the lakes in interior and northern British Columbia. Their operating hours are 8:30 AM to 4:00 PM daily.

The **Fraser Valley Hatchery** is located in Abbotsford. It raises native and domestic rainbow trout, anadromous and coastal cutthroat, and steelhead trout. It stocks some 150 lakes and streams each year in most of the regions in British Columbia. They maintain a captive-brood stock of the fish. The visitor center there offers displays and tours. The hours of operation are Monday through Friday, 8:00 AM to 3:00 PM.

The **Summerland Hatchery** is located on Okanogan Lake north of Penticton. It rears native and domestic rainbow trout. It is the oldest continuously running hatchery in British Columbia and is used to stock fish in some 260 lakes in the Thompson/Nicola, Okanogan, and West Kootenay regions. It also transfers fish to the Clearwater Hatchery for use in stocking the lakes in the Caribou and northern lake areas. During the three summer months of June, July, and August, free guided tours are available. Their hours of operation are 9:00 AM to 3:00 PM daily from April to September, and Monday through Friday from October to March.

The **Kootenay Hatchery** is located at Fort Steele near the town of Cranbrook. It is responsible for stocking 150 lakes in the east and west Kootenay regions as well as some of the lakes in the Kamloops and Okanogan regions. In addition, they transfer fish to the Clearwater Hatchery for central and northern stocking programs. Of special interest is their involvement in the recovery initiatives for white sturgeon.

Chapter 2

Special Information Can Give You an Edge

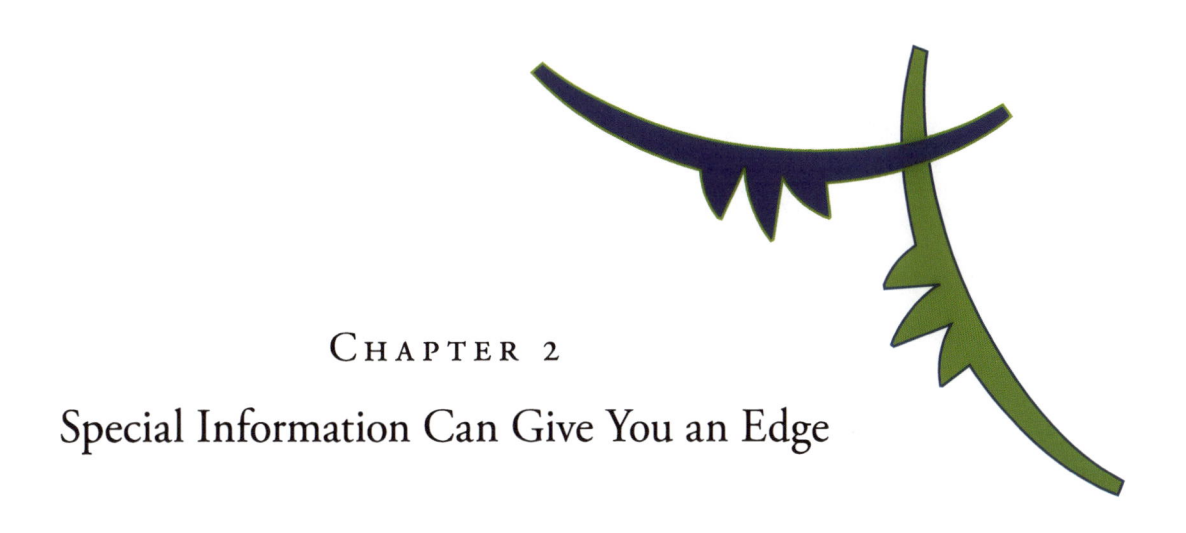

Fly fishers are a competitive bunch. They're always trying to outdo their fishing friends. Here are some tips to help you succeed.

Choosing the right place to fish can be very important. Basically fly fishers want to know where's the hot spot, how to get there, what facilities are available, and what fly patterns work there. Many folks will go back to a lake with which they are familiar and have fished previously. Much of the information in this book is specifically provided to help the fly fisher make the right choice.

Additional pieces of information are given in the following charts: "Fish Stocking Density /Acre" and "The Last Five years of Fish Stocking for Twenty-six of the Best Lakes." This data will help the angler figure out if it seems like there are lots of fish in a given lake, or if it's a spot where it is harder to catch a fish but is worth it because the fish are so large.

A note of caution in using this chart: there are many factors affecting the fishing in any one lake at any particular time, including weather, time of year, low water, wind, when the hatches are on, and whether the lake is in bloom. Then, too, take into account whether you're after big fish or lots of fish. As examples, if lots of fish are desired, a fly fisher may wish to try Eliguk Lake; if big fish are desired, the fisher should try one of the Triploid planted lakes.

One should also consider the factors of cost to make the trip, time and distance required, and facilities available. If a short weekend camping and fishing trip is desired, choose a lake that's not too many miles away and that has camping facilities and a boat launch area.

The "Fish Stocking Density/Acre" chart provides a snapshot as to what might be expected. Some special notes using 2009 data:

- Marquart Lake has 47 percent triploid brook trout, 53 percent diploid rainbows.

- Stump Lake has 22 percent Kokanee trout (half of those triploids), 78 percent rainbow trout (28 percent of which are triploids).

- Dragon Lake is stocked with rainbow trout only, and 40 percent of those are triploids.

- Minnie Lake and Stoney Lake levels have been raised in 2006 at a cost of $750,000, and the lakes were restocked at a cost of $500,000; there are 25,000 fish in each of the two lakes.

- Roche Lake is stocked with all rainbow trout, of which 33 percent are triploids.

- Tunkwa Lake is stocked with a total of 40,049 rainbow trout, of which 63 percent were female in 2009.

- Stump Lake has 100,000 Rainbows (40 percent triploids) and 80,000 Kokanee (50 percent triploids).

- Fawn Lake has the highest fish density/acre (189).

- This chart does not include fish from natural recruitment, which could be a major factor.

Fish Stocking Density in Twenty-six of the Best Lakes in BC
(T = Triploid) 2N= diploid, AF= all female, RB= rainbow, kok= kokanee

(BC Ministry of Environment)

Lake	Acres	Stocked 2009	Fish/Acre	Type
Badger	139	Natural spawn	unknown	Rainbow
Ballon	53	1500 T	28	Rainbow
Blue	30	2,000 T	66	Rainbow
Calling	74	6,000 2N	81 (2008)	Rainbow
Community	99	1,000 T	10	Rainbow
Corbett	72	Unknown	Well stocked	Rainbow
Dardanelles	120	2,000 T	17	Rainbow
Dragon	556	15,019 and 10,015 T	45	Rainbow
Eliguk	898	Natural	Many fish	Rainbow
Fawn	79	15,000 2N	189	Rainbow
Glimpse	259	15,000 2N	58	Rainbow
Hatheume	261	2,000 T	8	Rainbow
HiHium	865	20,356 2N (2008)	23 (2008)	Rainbow
Island (Big OK)	84	3,000 T	23	Rainbow
Janice	362	Natural spawn	unknown	Rainbow
Lac Le June	393	15,000 2N	38	Rainbow
Lundbom	114	3,013 T and 6,000 AF	79	Rainbow
Marquart	57	4,000 T and 4,500 2N	149	RB & brook
Minnie	300	Unknown	Well stocked	Rainbow
Peterhope	287	12,045 T	42	Rainbow
Plateau	96	7,000 2N	73	Rainbow
Roche	326	15,000 and 7,500 T	69	Rainbow
Stoney	About 150	Unknown	Well stocked	Rainbow
Stump	1928	40,000 T-rb 60,000 rb 40,000 T-kok 40,000 kok	93	55% RB 45% Kokanee
Sullivan	252	Natural	No data	Rainbow
Tunkwa	730	40,049	55	Rainbow

Last Five Years of Fish Planting for Twenty-six of the Best Lakes
(T = Triploid)

This chart shows total trout planted, including eastern brook in Marquart and kokanee in Stump Lake.

(BC Ministry of Environment)

Lake	2005	2006	2007	2008	2009
Badger	1,277 T	All native	All native	All native	All native
Ballon	1,500 T	1,500 T		1,500 T	1,500 T
Blue	2,000 T	2,000 T	2,000 T	2000 T	2,000 T
Calling	6,000	6,000	6,000	6,000	6,000 T
Community	1,000 T	3,000 T	1,000 T	1,000 T	1,000 T
Corbett	Private	Private	Private	Private	Private
Dardanelles	2,000 T	2,000	2,000 T	2,000 T	2,000 T
Dragon	33,304 & 10,033 T	35,126 & 10,000 T	15,046 & 10,261 T	14,999 10,079 T	15,019 10,015 T
Eliguk	All native	All native	All native	All native	All native
Fawn	15,000	15,000	15,000	15,000	15,000
Glimpse	7,000	15,000	15,000	15,000	15,000
Hatheume	3,500 T	3,500 T	3,500 T	3,500 T	2,000 T
HiHium	20,000	20,000	20,000	20,356	(Sept)
Janice	All native	All native	All native	All native	All native
Island (Big OK)	3,000 T	2,000 T	2,000 T	2,000 T	3,000 T
Lac Le Jeune	15,000	15,000	15,000	15,000	15,000
Lundbom	6,000	6,000	6,000 T	14,000	9,013 T
Marquart	4,500 T & 4,000	4,500 T& 4,000	4,500 T& 4,000	4,500 T & 4,000	4,000 T 4,500
Minnie	Private	25,000	Private	Private	Private
Peterhope	12,000	12,000	12,000	12,000 T	12,045 T
Plateau	8,000 & 2,000 T	8,000	8,000	8,000	7,000
Roche	15,000 & 7,500 T	15,000 & 17,500 T	15,000 & 7,500 T	14,993 & 7,496 T	15,000 & 7,500 T
Stoney	Private	25,000	Private	Private	Private
Stump	120,200 & 140,014 T	131,489 & 101,000 T	91,860 & 60,740 T	55,000 & 165,102 T	80,000 T & 100,000
Sullivan	All native	All native	All native	All native	All native
Tunkwa	35,000	25,074 & 15,000 T	25,164 & 15,000 T	39,989 20,000 AF	15,000 & 25,049 AF

Note: "All native" means no planting; natural reproduction.

The importance of this information is that it provides a guide to fly fishers as to exactly how each of the twenty-six best lakes in British Columbia have been stocked over the past five years, which should be an indicator of expectations. Note that natural recruitment will be in addition to the data shown and that it's important to review both the document titled "Fish Stocking Density/Acre" and the "Last Five Years of Fish Planting for Twenty-six of the Best Lakes."

Fish Finders and Depth Sounders

One of the more useful tools an angler can have is the fish finder. These devices can be mounted externally or internally on a boat, or they can be a portable handheld instrument.

The typical fish finder is battery operated either from separate batteries or from the same battery that powers an electric motor (twelve volts). A monitor is mounted in the boat where the screen can be seen by the operator. A transducer, usually mounted in the water off the transom of the boat, sends a cone-shaped beam down through the water that reads the water depth and sees any fish intercepted by the beam. (See the Lowrance X-55 scanner at the end of this chapter). Side scanners are also available. Various cone angles are available with many being a twenty-degree cone, but some have angles up to ninety degrees. The advantage of the larger cone angle is that the angler sees a larger area under the boat and thus can see more fish. Some fish finders show icons on the screen that discriminate as to large and small fish. If desired, a fish finder can be obtained that will read boat speed and water temperature.

My personal experience shows a twofold advantage to having a fish finder. First, when fishing a new lake or exploring a lake you are familiar with, the angler can troll or row the lake with the scanner switched on to locate pods of fish. Second, once this is done the angler can select a depth suitable for anchoring. One technique that works well is to anchor right on the edge of a drop-off so that casts can be made to deep water or up onto a bar or shallower area, all from the same anchored position. Double anchors (one front and one rear) are best when fishing the chironomid pattern. This holds the boat steady and helps the angler detect the soft "take" of the fly by the trout. Note that an eight-pound ball anchor seems to work best.

When mounting a fish finder in a boat, find a location for it that will minimize the number of times the fly line will get tangled up with it. There's some kind of a principle at work that proves if there is any slight protuberance in a boat, the fly line will find it!

Fish finders such as the X-55 have other features to help the angler. One is the backlight feature, which may be switched on in the evening to illuminate the screen. Another is an alarm that sounds when fish are located. And finally, some even play music for your entertainment.

The following photographs show both the portable and fixed fish finders.

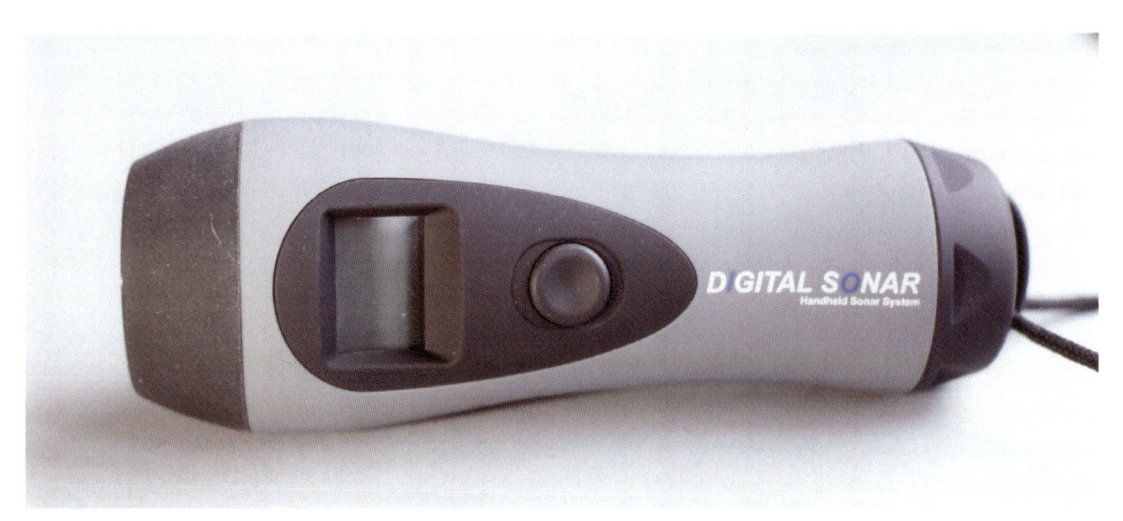

Norcross Marine Hawkeye Digital Hand Held Sonar System

This handheld fish finder is powered by four AA batteries. It is waterproof and is held underwater to read the depth and search for fish. It is lightweight, portable, and useful when traveling to lakes where to angler might not wish to take his electric motor and twelve-volt, deep-cycle battery equipment. It can be held so that it scans vertically or horizontally.

The Lowrance X-55 Fish Finder Sonar Unit (Mount on Boat Seat) and Transducer (Mount on Transom)

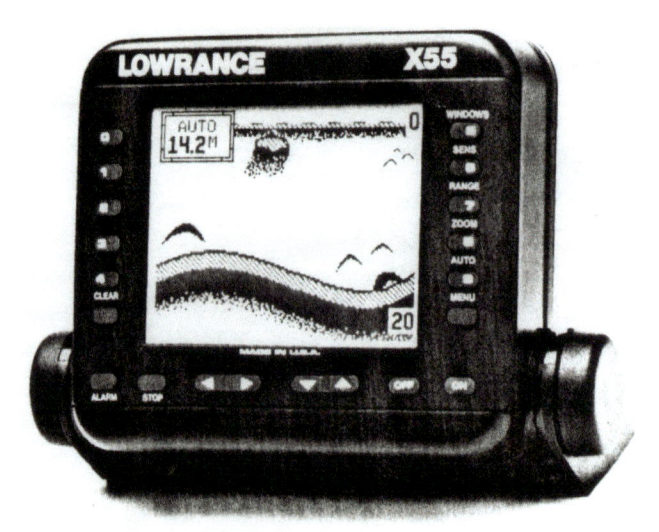

Fly Rods and Reels

There's an old saying that goes, "There is no such thing as too many fly rods or too many reels." To some extent this is true. Fly fishers are a competitive bunch, and it helps to have the right gear with you when you're out in a boat. That can mean not only having the right flies and gear in your tackle box, but also having the right rods and lines.

A system used by many experienced fly fishers who fish out of prams is to have along three or even four fly rods, each with a different type line. If the fly fisher is in a float tube or pontoon boat, there may be only room for one or two rods, but then extra reels can be taken, each loaded with a different fly line.

Because I fish out of a nine-foot pram most of the time, I usually bring three rods along: one with a floating line (WF6F or WF7F), one with a ten-foot sink tip line (WF6F/S type 3), and one with a sinking line (WF6S type 6). If a fourth rod is used, then two different rates of sinking lines can be used, one for shallower fishing and one for deeper waters. The advantage in doing this is that no time is wasted on switching lines; just pick up the desired rod and cast. It's a bit of a challenge to keep the rods from tangling with each other in the boat, but patience and persistence will solve the problem. Exploring a lake with a fish finder will usually reveal the depth where the fish are located. Then it's a matter of selecting the line that will place the fly at that depth.

The floating line has three general uses. One is to cast dry flies, and a second is to use for chironomid fishing where the boat is anchored and the cast is made with a leader long enough to let the fly sink to just above the bottom of the lake. In addition to these uses, a floating line with a nymph pattern just under the surface can be very effective.

Sink tip lines are great for casting up onto shoals and bars where feeding fish are often seen. Various sink rates for the sinking section are available, but two are my favorites. One is the WF7F/S type 3 the other a WF6F/S type 3, which work well for most occasions. But sometimes a slow-sinking-tip line can be the ticket because it will put the fly down to a shallower depth.

Sinking lines—some folks refer to these as full sinking lines—are just the thing for fishing deeper waters. For general exploration of a lake, a type 4 or type 6 sink rate seem to work best. I prefer a type 6 when the water depth is twenty-five feet or more. Another use for sinking lines is to fish the chironomid when the fish finder shows the fish are deep, thirty to forty feet or more. Then, providing the angler has a long enough anchor rope, the sinking line will put the fly right down to where the trout are.

Fishing in the Evening

In the springtime Kamloops trout have a propensity to be especially active in the evening. Often the best action is between 7:30 PM and 11:00 PM, and many fly fishers quit too early. This later time does have the advantage that those folks who troll with hardware are usually off the lake, making it less crowded. In the months of May and June and into the early parts of July, there will be a sedge (caddis) hatch every evening.

This hatch occurs on the shoals and bars in shallow waters that are anywhere from two to ten feet deep. It's a challenge for the fly fisher because it may be so dark out that you can see neither the rise nor your fly. Yet the fish are there and are active, especially the big fish.

It seems the larger fish will move into the shoals and up onto the bars to partake of an evening repast of juicy caddis morsels. One of the better ways to hook up with these trout is to use a floating fly line with a Tom Thumb, Grizzly King, or Black O'Lindsay on the end of a nine-foot leader. Other sedge fly patterns will work too. Then simply mooch the fly along on top of the shoal very slowly and hang on! The strike will be a heart stopper. Be certain that your rod is secured in the boat or it'll be lost overboard.

If it's just dusk and isn't quite dark yet, rising fish can be spotted if the water is calm, and they can be cast to. But after dark it's another matter. This presents another situation where a fish finder can be very useful. Many fish finders have a feature called backlighting, where the screen is illuminated so that the angler can see how deep the water is where the angler is fishing even when the sky is pitch black. Often fish will be taken in very shallow water because the sedges seem to migrate toward the shore. Evidence of this is found in the morning, when anglers go down to the dock where their boats are moored and see caddis shucks or adults in, on, and around their boats.

A technique that is successful is to start the evening with a sink tip line and then switch to a floating line when dusk settles in. It's also essential to have a small flashlight along. It'll help you after dark to see into your tackle box, to untangle snarls, or to tie on a new fly.

SUCCESSFUL FISHING TECHNIQUES
1. Using the Sinking Line

One of the most useful and successful sinking lines is the type 6 full sinking line. The Cortland 444 type six weight forward line (WF6S type 6) is a favorite. A technique that really works when exploring a lake or when looking for big trout is to use this line in combination with a fish finder or depth finder. It seems that it works best when in water depths of twenty to thirty-five feet because many of the big fish cruise along the bottom to feed. Follow the contours of the lake to stay at a consistent depth. To reach the level where the fish are, when mooching the fly (rowing slowly), it's necessary to put the entire line in the water. It's amazing how many times this works compared to the anglers who are fishing a type 3 or type 4 sinking line. True, you'll get some weeds on the line now and then, so it's a good idea to check the fly often, especially if you think you've had a strike or connected with a weed.

British Columbia fishing regulations have permitted anglers fishing alone in a boat on a lake to use two lines. This presents a bit of a challenge to keep them untangled or from having one sink to the bottom while playing a fish on the other. But the advantage is that two different sink rate lines can be used at once, such as a type 6 and a type 3 or a sink tip. In that way the angler finds out at what depth the fish are located.

2. Using the Sink Tip

Sink tip lines are available in many types and lengths. One of the most productive for lake fishing is a 5, 6, or 7 weight with a ten-foot sinking section. It can be used while either trolling or casting. As an example, the Cortland WF7F/S type 3 with a ten-foot sinking section is perfect for fishing shallow waters. Anchor the boat in about six to eight feet of water, near the edge of a drop-off. Using that technique the angler will be able to cast up onto the shoal and begin an immediate retrieve, or he can cast into deeper water and let the fly sink before retrieving. Be sure to try casting the fly to the deep water, letting it sink and then bringing it up the side of the drop-off. Fish will cruise along the edge of a drop-off. This technique seems to work best in daylight hours; at night it's another story.

3. Using the Floating Line

Sometimes fish are active in very shallow water, especially during a hatch. A floating line such as a 5, 6, or 7 weight can be just the ticket. A WF7F works well depending on the rod design. Not only can this line be used to fish dry flies to match the hatch, but it can also be used to fish nymphs or chironomids. A leader length of nine feet will help to keep from spooking the fish.

4. Regardless of Which Line Is Used

The full thrill of the strike can occur only with the rod in the angler's hand. This condition will give a better chance to hook and land the fish, and it is certainly the most fun!

THE LONG-HANDLED NET

It's amazing to see how many anglers miss out on the advantages of using a long-handled net, such as the one shown above. It was made by my longtime friend, craftsman and fly fisher Theron Chamberlain. This is especially true when fishing from a boat. There's nothing quite as disappointing as not being able to land a big fish because you can't get it close enough to the boat or the net is too small. Both of those problems can be taken care of by using a net with a generously long handle. It's a simple and inexpensive way to up the odds of being able to handle a large fish.

Many commercially made nets are made for the stream fisher where portability is a major factor. These nets typically have very short handles. But nets are made in all types of configurations: some have wooden frames, some are plastic, some are aluminum, some are collapsible. The trick here is to purchase a "boat net." These are typically forty to fifty inches long overall with a net bag of about fifteen inches by twenty-one and a half inches. Remember too that these bags can be attained in rubber rather than nylon or synthetic material. The rubber net bags are much gentler on the fish, making the safe release of the fish easier and better.

If a local wood worker who makes nets is available, simply specify a long-handled net with a generously sized rubber bag. Some of these custom nets are beautiful works of art and a treasure for the angler.

The boat angler will find this type of net much easier to use either standing or sitting. It's a bit safer to keep the boat from overturning or swamping because the angler doesn't have to reach so far out.

Understanding What It Means When a Lake "Turns Over"

For a long time I thought that folks who claimed a lake turned over were just full of baloney and simply had another excuse why fishing wasn't good. But I learned I was wrong. Here's an explanation as to what really happens:

First of all, the answer is rooted in the actual scientific characteristics of water. It turns out that the density of water varies with temperature and that it reaches its maximum density at 39.16 degrees Fahrenheit. Now consider what happens when a frozen lake thaws out in the spring, as many of the lakes in British Columbia do. The surface temperature when frozen is 32 degrees, but as the lake thaws in the springtime, the temperature of the water on the upper surface gradually warms up. When the surface water reaches 39.16, it reaches maximum density, so it is heavier than the water below it and sinks. This is what is meant by the term "spring turnover."

As this process continues, the lake mixes and stratifies into three layers. The upper layer is called the epilimnion, the middle layer is called the metalimnion, and the bottom layer is known as the hypolimnion. Within the middle layer of a stratified lake there is a horizontal band known as the thermocline. This layer contains the proper characteristics of temperature and dissolved oxygen to be favorable to trout. Usually the temperature of the thermocline favorable to trout is between 54–65 degrees (some references say 60–70 degrees). What the fly fisher needs to do is to find out how far down the thermocline layer is and fish in that zone. That's why fly lines with different sink rates are useful: the right one can put you in the zone.

As you might expect, the reverse happens in the fall. The surface of the lake cools down gradually until it reaches 39.16 degrees and sinks once more. This phenomenon is known as the "fall turnover." The lake continues to cool down until the surface freezes.

Generally speaking, fishing is not particularly good during a turnover, but it improves once stratification has occurred.

Chapter 3

26 of the Best Lakes in British Columbia

This chapter is devoted to guiding fly fishers to proven lakes in British Columbia that produce great fishing. There are hundreds of lakes from which to choose, but select one of these and you'll have a good chance of a successful trip. The description of each of these lakes includes how to find it, where it is, how it has been stocked, how large the lake is, what the elevation is, what flies work there, and what regulations apply.

BADGER LAKE

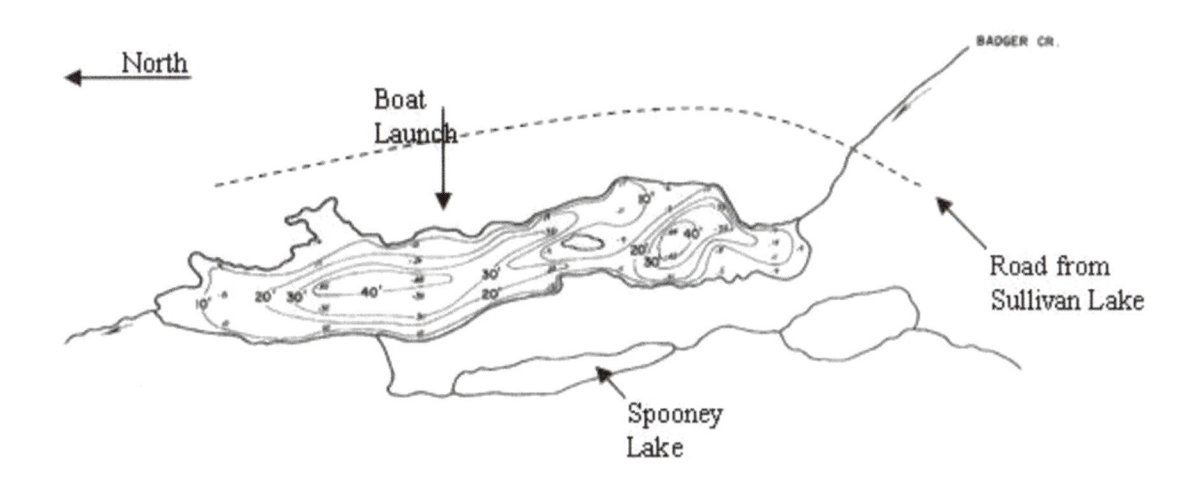

Gazetted name: Badger Lake (Source: BC Ministry of Environment)

Badger Lake is a beautiful but small lake located at an elevation of 3546 feet and only about 4 miles north of Knouff (Sullivan) Lake. To get there, take Highway 5 north from the city of Kamloops about 14 miles. Turn right onto the Heffley-Louis Creek Road, travel about 5 miles, and then turn left onto a secondary road that leads past Knouff Lake and continues north to Badger Lake. This lake is oriented north and south and has two deep spots of about 40 feet, one on the north end of the lake and the other toward the south end of the lake.

General location: Northeast of Kamloops
Surface area: 139 acres
Elevation: 3546 feet
Maximum depth: 40 feet
Regulations: (readers consult latest issue)
1. No fishing December 1 through April 30
2. Bait ban
3. Single barbless hooks

The lake has been quite well-known for its big fish. Badger Lake was not stocked in the years 1995–2004. It did receive a plant of 1,277 triploids in 2005 but was not stocked in 2006–2009. Badger Lake is known for good chironomid hatches in the spring and sedge flies in June. See the chapter on flies for the Tom Thumb, the Grizzly King, and Black O'Lindsay patterns for sedges, as well as the Ice Cream Cone pattern for chironomids.

The boat launching area is quite nice and is located on the east side of the lake about halfway along the length.

To review the fish planting history of Badger Lake, see the chart below.

| Badger Lake Stocking History ||||
| T = Triploid ||||
Year	# Fish Planted	Year	# Fish Planted
1932	900	1973	12,000
1937	5000	1974	28,000
1938	15,000	1975	4,000
1939	30,000	1976	5,000
1940	5,000	1977	8,000
1965	8,000	1988	8,000
1966	18,000	1979	4,000
1967	18,000	1980	4,000
1968	16,000	1990	4,000
1969	16,000	1991	2,000
1970	16,000	1994	2,500
1971	5,000	2005	1277 T
1972	12,000		None since

Badger Lake Looking North

Note: Spooney Lake is located just to the west of Badger Lake and holds smaller fish, but it is also worth a visit.

BALLON LAKE

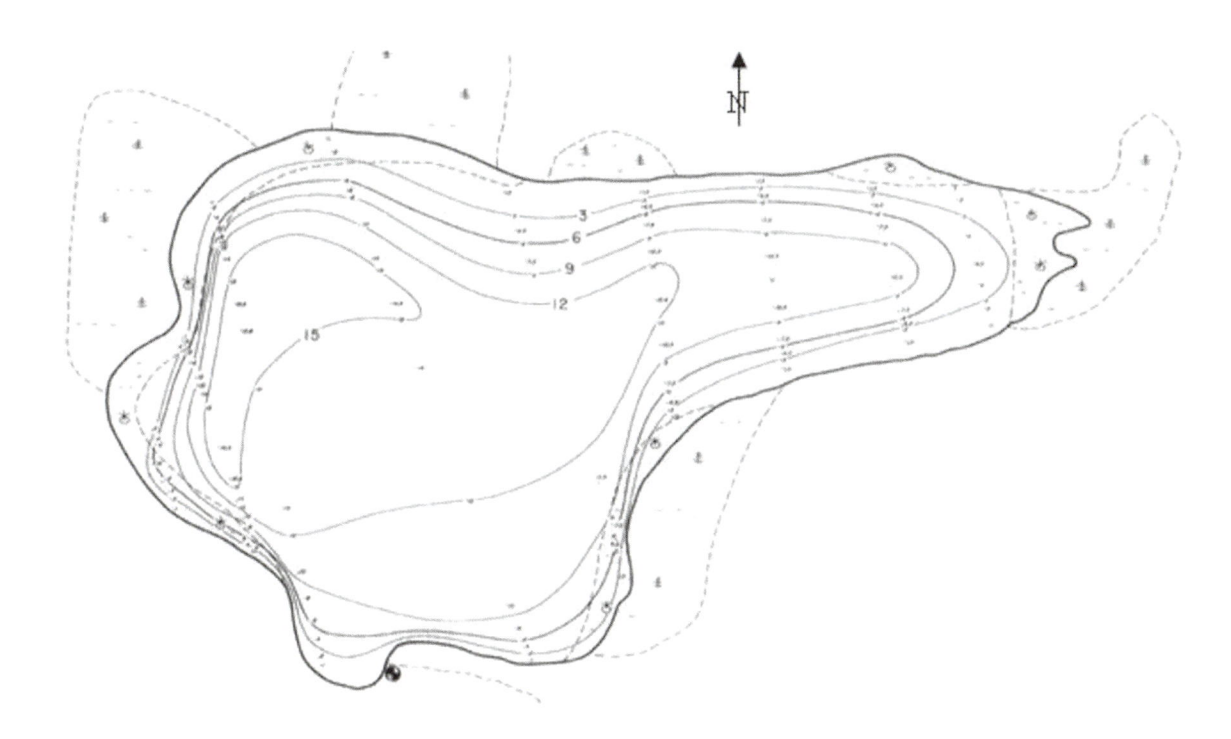

Ballon Lake is a small lake located in the Caribou region northwest of Horsefly. To get there, take Highway 97 north toward Williams Lake. At the 150-mile house, turn right on the road that goes to Likely and Horsefly and then take the Beaver Valley Road until just before Roberts Lake is reached. At that point turn left and go south on a dirt road leading to Ballon Lake. Note that a good place to stay overnight is at the campgrounds or motels in the nearby town of Lac La Hache.

This lake was first recommended to me by Jeb Sires. He has fished it a number of years with great success and often caught trout of twenty inches or more. Access is difficult but possible and may require carrying a boat a short way down to the shore.

Gazetted name: Ballon Lake (Source: BC Ministry of Environment)
General location: Northwest of Horsefly
Surface area: 53 acres
Elevation: 2575 feet
Maximum depth: about 52 feet
Regulations: (readers consult current issue)
  1. Catch and release only
  2. Bait ban
  3. Single barbless hook
  4. Closed to fishing November 1 through April 30

Ballon Lake is a small lake of only fifty-three acres. Its deepest spot (fifty-two feet) is located roughly in the northwest part of the lake. Ballon Lake has good weed beds that produce good damsel fly hatches each June. This lake has special regulations. Ballon Lake has been planted with triploid trout during 2005–2009 as shown on the following plant summary chart. This alone should make it worth a visit.

Ballon Lake Fish Stocking History

Ballon Lake Stocking History			
Year			
	Fish Planted Diploids	Fish Planted Triploids	Size
1990	1400		Yearling
1991	1800		Yearling
1995	3914		Fry
1996	2000		Fry
1997	3000		Fry
1998	3000		Fry
1999	2000		Fry
2000	1500		Fry
2001		1500	Fry
2002		1500	Fry
2004		1000	Fingerling
2005		1500	Fingerling/fry
2006		1500	Fry
2007		1500	Fry
2008		1500	Fry
2009		1500	Fry

BLUE LAKE

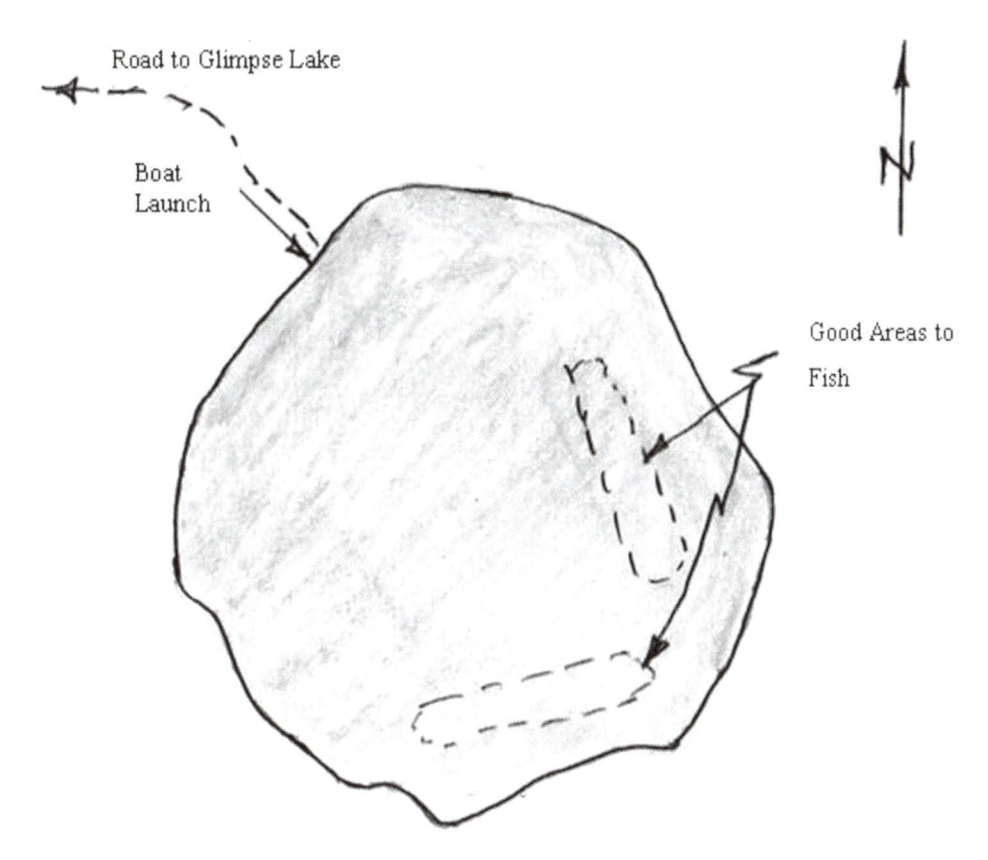

Blue Lake is a beautiful but very small body of water located about two miles by road northeast of Glimpse Lake. The road to it does have a mud hole or two that can be a challenge in bad weather, so a truck is advised. It is a lovely spot, though there are no cabins, resorts, or facilities at the lake.

Blue Lake is lightly planted, as can be seen in the following fish stocking history, but it does produce some big fish for the patient angler. Province regulations make this one of the treasured fly fishing–only lakes in British Columbia.

Along with my fly fishing partners, Wilbur Watson and Maury Skeith, I have been fishing this lake for some thirty-seven years and have taken some lovely trout up to seven and a half pounds. Flies that work here include the Leecherous Dragon, the Nyerges Nymph, the Black O'Lindsay, and of late the chironomid (Ice Cream Cone).

Gazetted name: Blue Lake (Source: BC Ministry of Environment)

General location: 2 miles from Glimpse Lake

Surface area: 30 acres

Elevation: About 4000 feet

Maximum depth: about 30 feet

Regulations (reader consult current issue).
 1. Closed to fishing Dec 1 through April 30
 2. Daily limit: 2 fish
 3. Fly fishing only, single barbless hook
 4. Bait ban

Note that the planting history of this lake reveals that triploids have been planted every year beginning in 1996, with the exception of 2004. The plant quantity is small, but fish have been taken up to thirteen pounds, making it worthwhile. Please see the following chart:

Blue Lake Fish Stocking History Lake 00111NICL							
Year	Diploid	Triploid	Size	Year	Diploid	Triploid	Size
1976	2,000			1993	3,000		Fall Fry
1977	2,000			1994	3,000		Fall Fry
1978	2,000			1995	3,000		Fall Fry
1979	2,000			1996		2,000	Fall Fry
1981	2,000			1997		2,000	Fry
1983	3,000			1998		2,000	Fall Fry
1984	3,000			1999		2,000	Fall Fry
1985	3,000			2000		2,000	Fry
1986	3,000			2002		2,000	Yearling
1987	3,000			2003		2,000	Yearling
1988	3,000			2004	2,000		Yearling
1990	3,000		Fall Fry	2005		2,000	Yearling
1991	3,000		Fall Fry	2006		2,000	Yearling
1992	3,000		Fall Fry	2007		2,000	Yearling
				2008		2,000	Yearling
				2009		2,000	Yearling

Blue Lake with Dick Hankinson and Wil Watson at boats

CALLING LAKE

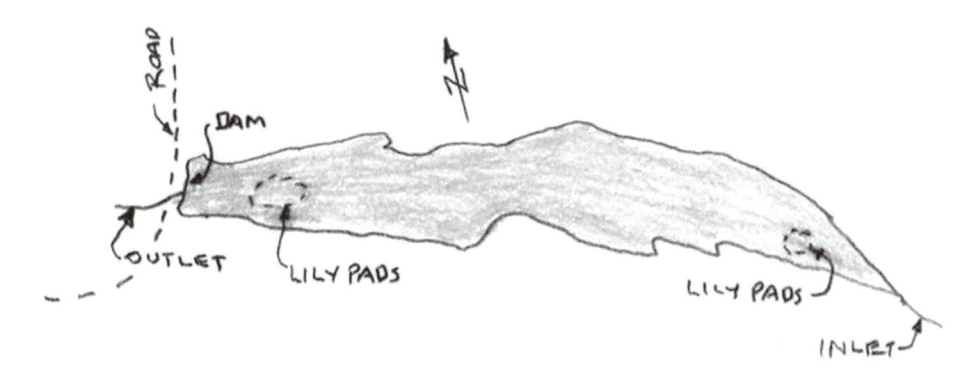

Calling Lake is a picturesque, high mountain lake located west of the town of Logan Lake. It is situated at an elevation of 5,281 feet and is surrounded by woodlands. To reach the lake, drive west on Highway 97C past the Highland Valley copper mine and its tailings pond, then turn left onto the Laura Lake road. This road passes through the Highland Valley mine property and leads to both Big OK Lake and Calling Lake. The road is reasonably well marked, but it is not maintained and is very rough, with lots of pot holes.

There is an earthen dam at the outlet of the lake where the boat launch and forestry campsite are located. The inlet is located at the opposite end of the lake from the boat launch. Calling Lake is fairly small, being only seventy-four acres in size, and it is a long, fairly narrow lake. It receives a plant of about six thousand fry each fall.

Gazetted name: Calling Lake (Source: BC Ministry of Environment)

General location: West of Logan Lake

Surface area: 74 acres

Elevation: 5281 feet

Maximum depth: about 45 feet

Regulations: (readers consult current issue)
1. Bait ban
2. Single barbless hook
3. Daily limit: 2 fish

Left to right: author, Roger Hutchings, Maury Skeith, Hugh Clark

On occasion there will be a fine sedge hatch, during which fish rise well to the Tom Thumb dry fly. Other times good flies include Watson's Anomaly and the Nyerges Nymph. Some of the better areas to fish include all along the north shore, the area around the lily pads (shallow water) near the boat launch, and the far end of the lake near the inlet where another lily pad cluster is found. The best time of the year seems to be in July because the lake is quite high in elevation, but this depends a great deal on the weather.

	Calling Lake Stocking History				
Year	Fish Planted Diploids	Stage		Year	Fish Planted Diploids	Stage
1932	10,000	Eggs		1998	6,000	Fall Fry
1985	6,000			1999	6,000	Fall Fry
1988	6,000			2000	6,000	Fry
1989	5,000	Fall Fry		2001	6,000	Fry
1990	4,000	Fall Fry		2002	6,000	Fry
1991	4,000	Fall Fry		2003	6,000	Fry
1992	4,000	Fall Fry		2004	6,000	Fry
1993	4,000	Fall Fry		2005	6,000	Fry
1994	4,000	Fall Fry		2006	6,000	Fry
1995	4,000	Fall Fry		2007	6,000	Fry
1996	6,000	Fall Fry		2008	6,000	Fry
1997	6,000	Fall Fry		2009	6,000	Fry

Photograph of Calling Lake from boat launch area

COMMUNITY LAKE

← TO HEFFLEY CREEK ROAD

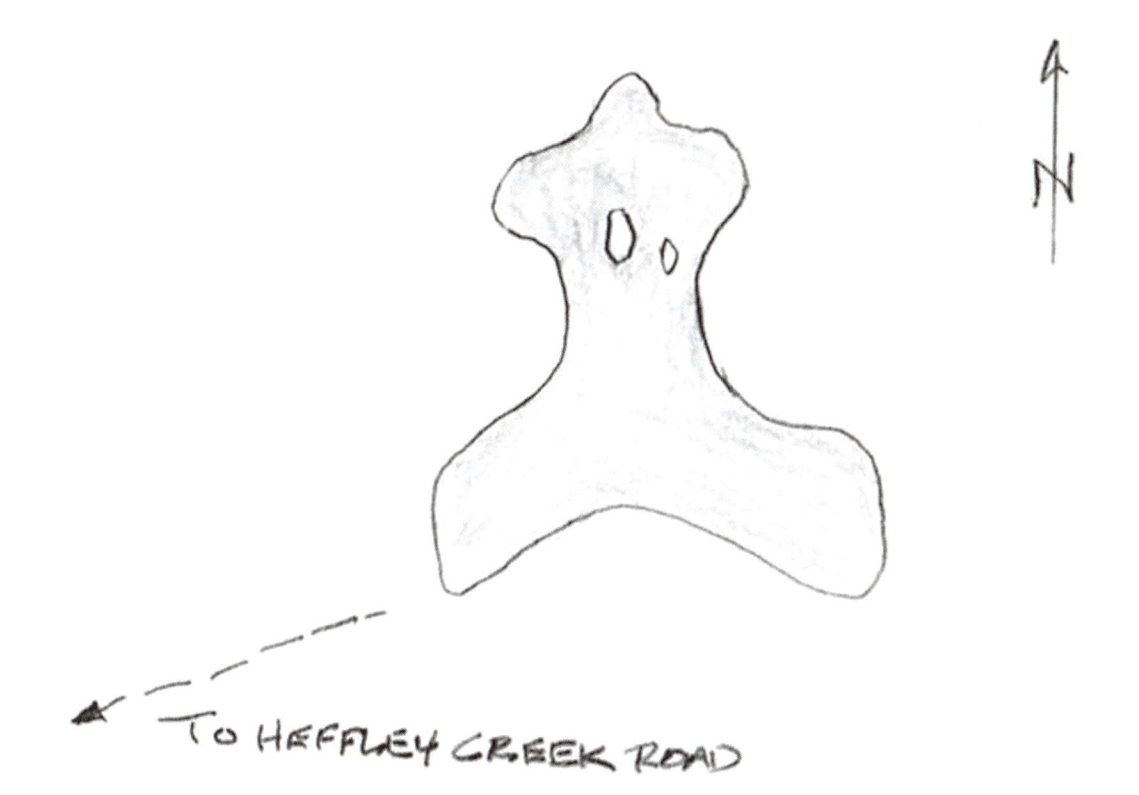

Community Lake is a small lake located northeast of the city of Kamloops. To get there, take Highway 5 north from Kamloops for thirteen miles, then turn right onto the Heffley Creek Road. Travel four and a half miles and take the left fork for another four and a half miles onto a road that eventually leads past Sullivan Lake (also known as Knouff), then turn right and go three miles on a road east to Community Lake.

Here's a lake that is a good example of how a small lake declines as a desired spot once the word is out. While Community Lake was still relatively unknown, it was a good fishery. But nowadays fishing pressure is intense, and anglers may be disappointed. Eight new camping spots have recently been added by the forest service in addition to the original boat-launching and camping area. The lake level is controlled by a locked gate valve on the weir at the outlet, but as with many of the lakes in the Kamloops area, the lake level is down about two to three feet, adding to its problems.

A campsite with boat launch is provided. The best time to fish this lake is in the spring or early summer. This lake has a good sedge fly hatch in June, so the Tom Thumb is a popular dry fly to use. Two other good patterns for

> Gazetted name: Community Lake (Source BC Ministry of Environment)
>
> General location: 25 miles northeast of Kamloops
>
> Surface Area: 99 acres
>
> Elevation: 4559 feet
>
> Regulations: (readers consult current issue)
>   1. No fishing December 1 through April 30
>   2. Limit: 2 trout daily
>   3. Bait ban
>   4. Single barbless hook

the sedge hatch are the Grizzly King and the Black O'Lindsay. Anglers proficient in the use of chironomids and leeches also have good success. Tying descriptions are available in the chapter "Must Have Flies."

What is unusual about this lake is that it has a thirteen-year history of having been planted with triploid trout. The plant is small in numbers but has produced some lovely large trout. Much of the lake has pronounced marl shoals as well, but there are two deep pools (one in the northeast end and one in the northwest end), and some islands to add to its intrigue. What has affected this lake is too much pressure for too few fish. Too many anglers worked over this small lake during the past ten years; most likely it will never be the same again. Although it is a lovely spot, it is often crowded with little to offer in the way of solitude. Whenever a reasonably good lake is this close to a major city, heavy fishing pressure can be anticipated and the secret always gets out.

The area does offer some other choices; two good lakes nearby are Sullivan Lake (Knouff) and Badger Lake. See the following chart for the stocking history of Community Lake; pay special attention to the years 1996–2008. Note too that in the chapter "To Get an Edge," the chart titled "Fish Stocking Density per Acre" shows that Community Lake has the lowest fish density of all the lakes shown. This means the angler will have to work in order to find a fish.

Community Lake Stocking History						
Year	Fish Planted Diploids	Size	Year	Fish Planted Diploids	Triploids	Fish Planted Size
1924	2500	Fry	1989	3,000		Yearlings
1969	15,000	Fry	1990	5,000		Yearlings
1870	15,000	Fry	1991	3,500		Yearlings
1971	15,000	Fry	1992	2,500		Yearlings
1972	15,000	Fry	1993	2,500		Yearlings
1973	15,000	Fry	1994	2,500		Yearlings
1974	5,000	Fry	1995	2,500		Yearlings
1975	10,000	Fry	1996	2,500		Yearlings
1976	8,000		1997		2,500	Yearlings
1977	8,000		1998		2,500	Yearlings
1978	8,000		1999		2,500	Yearlings
1979	6,000		2000		2,500	Yearlings
1980	8,000		2001		2,000	Yearlings
1982	8,000		2002		2,000	Yearlings
1983	5,000		2003		2,000	Yearlings
1984	5,000		2004		2,000	Yearlings
1985	5,000		2005		1,000	Yearlings
1986	5,000		2006		3,000	Fingerling/yearling
1987	4,000		2007		1,000	Yearlings
1988	4,000		2008		1,000	Yearlings
			2009		1,000	Yearlings

CORBETT LAKE

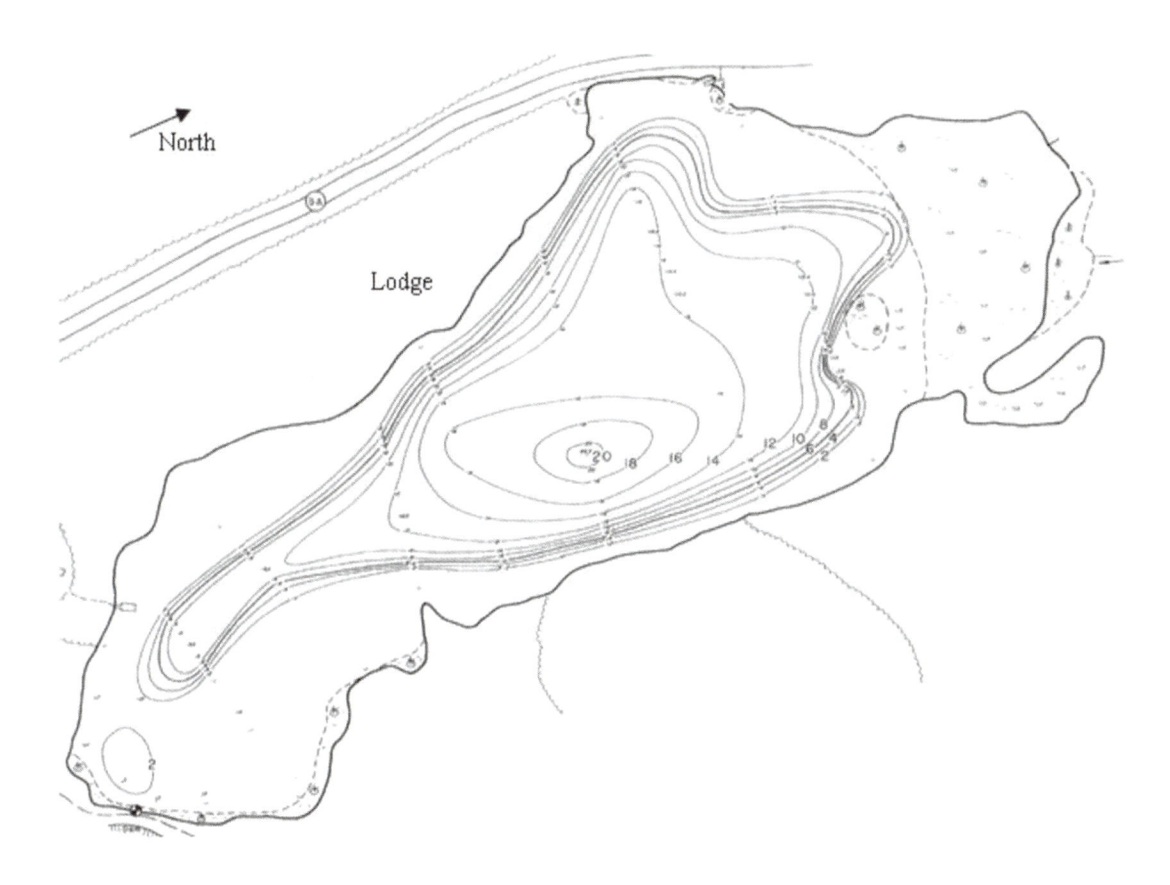

Corbett Lake is located alongside Highway 97C about twelve miles southeast of the town of Merritt. This lake is privately controlled by Peter McVey, who owns and operates the Corbett Lake Country Inn Resort. The lake is well-known to fly fishers and produces very large trout each year. Peter controls the only access to the lake through his property and stocks the lake himself. The resort provides cabins, rooms, meals, and boats.

To keep this lake from having a fish kill over the winter, an aerator is utilized. Although not confirmed yet, one source indicates that 3,275 fish were planted in the lake recently by private stocking. Corbett Lake was last planted by the government in 1993.

Fishing with a chironomid is good in this lake, particularly in the north end of the lake, although many other patterns work as well. Good times to fish here are in May, June, early July, and September.

Those who have visited the Corbett Lake Country Inn have enjoyed the very fine meals prepared by cordon bleu

Gazetted name: Corbett Lake (Source: BC Ministry of Environment)

General location: 12 miles southeast of Merritt

Surface area: 71.7 acres

Elevation: 3417 feet

Maximum depth: 67 feet

Regulations: (readers consult latest issue)
 1. Closed to fishing December 1 through April 30
 2. Daily limit: 2 fish
 3. Bait ban
 4. Single barbless hook
 5. Fly fishing only

chef Peter McVey. That alone makes a trip to this spot worthwhile. Another special event hosted by Peter McVey, which I have attended regularly, is the Bamboo Rod Builder's Workshop, a four-day event held in April biennially since 1988. This workshop brings craftsmen from all over the world and is considered the premier bamboo rod builder's event.

The Corbett Lake Country Inn

DARDANELLES LAKE

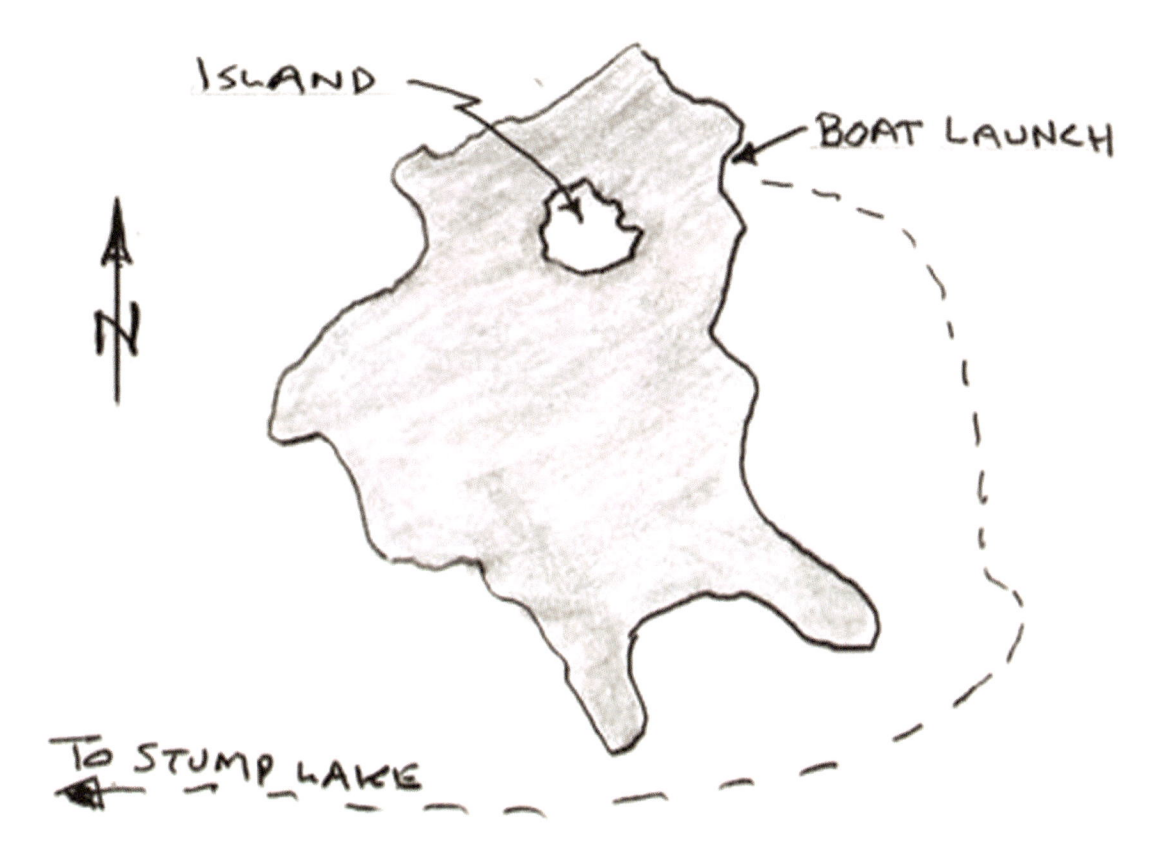

Dardanelles is somewhat unknown lake by U.S. fly fishers but is well-known to the Canadians. It is a relatively small lake but is quite beautiful and fairly difficult to find. The lake is located about six miles as the crow flies (about nine miles by road) due east of Stump Lake. Take Highway 5A north out of Merritt and turn east at the north end of Stump Lake. It's a dirt road all the way with several forks, so it's best to have a map of the area to keep from getting lost.

Dardanelles does have a small campground and boat launch area. In earlier years it was stocked with ten thousand fry in 1960 and again in 1984. Since then the annual stocking leveled off at four thousand fry in the years 1991–1999. Of special interest is that Dardanelles has been stocked with two thousand triploids each year from 2001–2009.

The best fishing seems to be with the spring hatches in May and June. Please refer to the following chart for the stocking history of this lake.

> Gazetted name: Dardanelles Lake (Source: BC Ministry of Environment)
> General location: East of Stump Lake
> Surface area: 120 acres
> Regulations: (readers consult current issue)
>   1. Limit: 2 fish daily
>   2. Bait ban
>   3. Single barbless hook

Dardanelles Lake Stocking History							
Year	Diploid	Triploid	Stage	Year	Diploid	Triploid	Stage
1960	10,000		Fry	1997	4,000		Fry
1984	10,000			1998	4,000		Fall Fry
1985	5000			1999	4,000		Fall Fry
1986	8,000			2000	2,000		Fry
1987	8,000			2001		3,000	Fry
1990	6,000		Fall Fry	2002		3,000	Fry
1991	4,000		Fall Fry	2003		3,000	Fry
1992	4,000		Fall Fry	2004		2,000	Fry
1993	4,000		Fall Fry	2005		2,000	Fry
1994	4,000		Fall Fry	2006		2,000	Fry
1995	4,000		Fall Fry	2007		2,000	Fry
1996	4,000		Fall Fry	2008		2,000	Fry
				2009		2,000	Fry

LeaAnn Gould at Dardanelles Lake

DRAGON LAKE

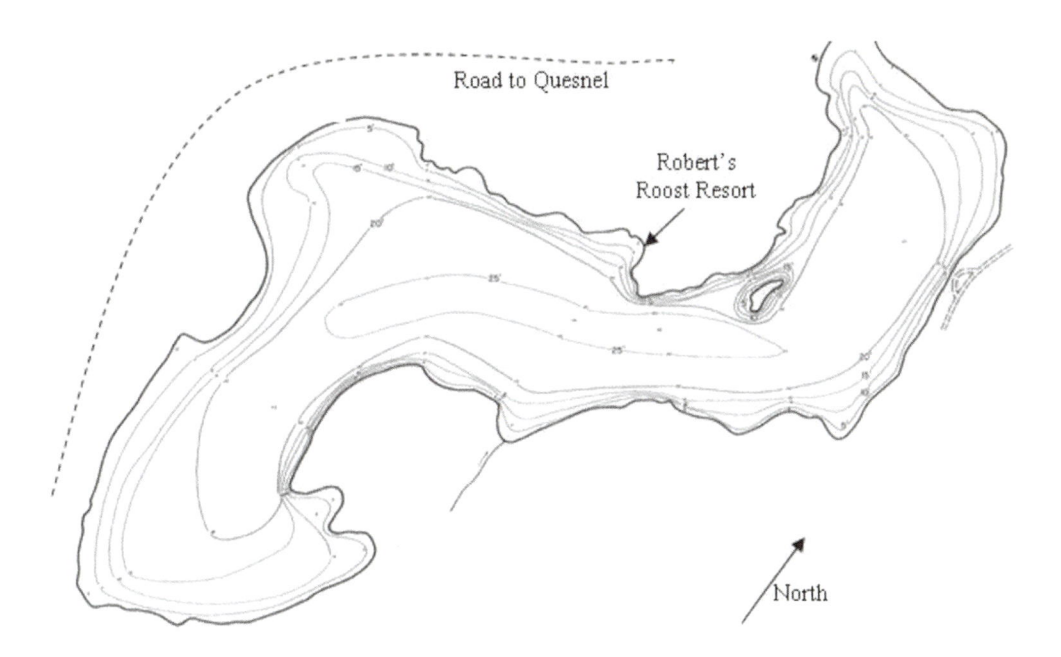

Now here's a lake every fly fisher should try his or her skills on! Dragon is known for its 12-pound trout (although I had to settle for 11.5). Dragon is located right alongside Highway 97 some 2.6 miles south of the town Quesnel. It's a long drive (320 miles north of the town of Hope) for most folks, and fishing pressure is high, but it is well worth the time and effort.

Dragon Lake is fairly large at 556, acres but gas outboards are allowed. It has a well-developed resort including trailer hook-ups, a washroom, and a laundromat located on the east side of the lake. Public boat launches can be found on the east and north sides.

Dragon has been heavily planted since 1927 and now includes some triploids. These fish grow rapidly and reach very large size. The creek entering Dragon Lake is used as an egg-stripping station so that these eggs may be used to plant in other lakes. Fishing is good in May and June and then slows in the hot summer months before it is good again in September and October. Best patterns include chironomids, Leeches, Wooly Buggers, Damsel Nymphs, and Dragon Fly Nymphs. Try the flats to find feeding fish, and then fish the deeper areas by the island. Anchoring and casting with a sinking line works well, as does trolling.

> Gazetted name: Dragon Lake (Source: BC Ministry of Environment)
> General location: 2.6 miles south of Quesnel
> Surface area: 556 acres
> Elevation: 1900 feet
> Maximum depth: 26 feet
> Regulations: (readers consult current issue)
>   1. Daily limit: 1 fish
>   2. No fishing between signs on opposite shores of Hallis Creek.

A summary of the fish planting history of Dragon Lake is shown on the following chart. Note in particular the huge number of fish planted in 1963 and 1964 (over three hundred thousand each year). Then since 1989 the plant consisted of some yearlings instead of just fry. A substantive change was initiated in the year 2000 when triploids were introduced into the lake along with the regular diploids. Note that the all-female triploids are sterile fish and do not propagate, but they do grow to immense size.

Dragon Lake Stocking History							
Year	Diploid	Size		Year	Diploid	Triploid	Size
1927	50,000	Eggs		1987	45,028		
1956	25,000	Fry		1988	55,908		
1963	342,000	Fry		1989	51,000		Yearling/Fry
1964	300,000	Fry		1990	48,311		Yearling/Fry
1965	40,000	Fry		1991	60,000		Yearling/Fry
1967	10,000	Fry		1992	50,000		Yearling/Fry
1967	50,400	Fingerling Brook Trout		1993	50,000		Yearlings
1968	50,000	Fry		1994	30,000		Yearlings
1969	77,000	Fry		1995	39,985		Yearlings
1970	40,000	Fry		1996	31,024		Yearlings
1971	30,000	Fry		1997	30,195		Yearlings
1973	45,000	Fry		1998	35,010		Yearlings
1974	40,000	Fry		1999	35,524		Yearlings
1975	45,000	Fry		2000	40,688	5,093	Yearling/Fry
1976	50,000			2001	35,334	5,090	Yearling/Fry
1977	40,000			2002	35,108	5,010	Yearling/Fingerling
1978	49,365			2003	37,257	5,052	Yearling/Fry
1970	10,000			2004	45,716	5,012	Yearling/Fry
1980	25,000			2005	33,304	10,033	Yearling/Fry
1981	35,000			2006	35,126	10,000	Yearling/Fry
1982	35,000			2007	14,474	10,261	Yearlings
1983	45,000			2008	15,000	10,079	Yearlings
1984	40,000			2009	15,000	10,050	Yearlings
1985	30,000						
1986	65,000						

The author with an 11.5-pound Kamloops trout from Dragon Lake

ELIGUK LAKE

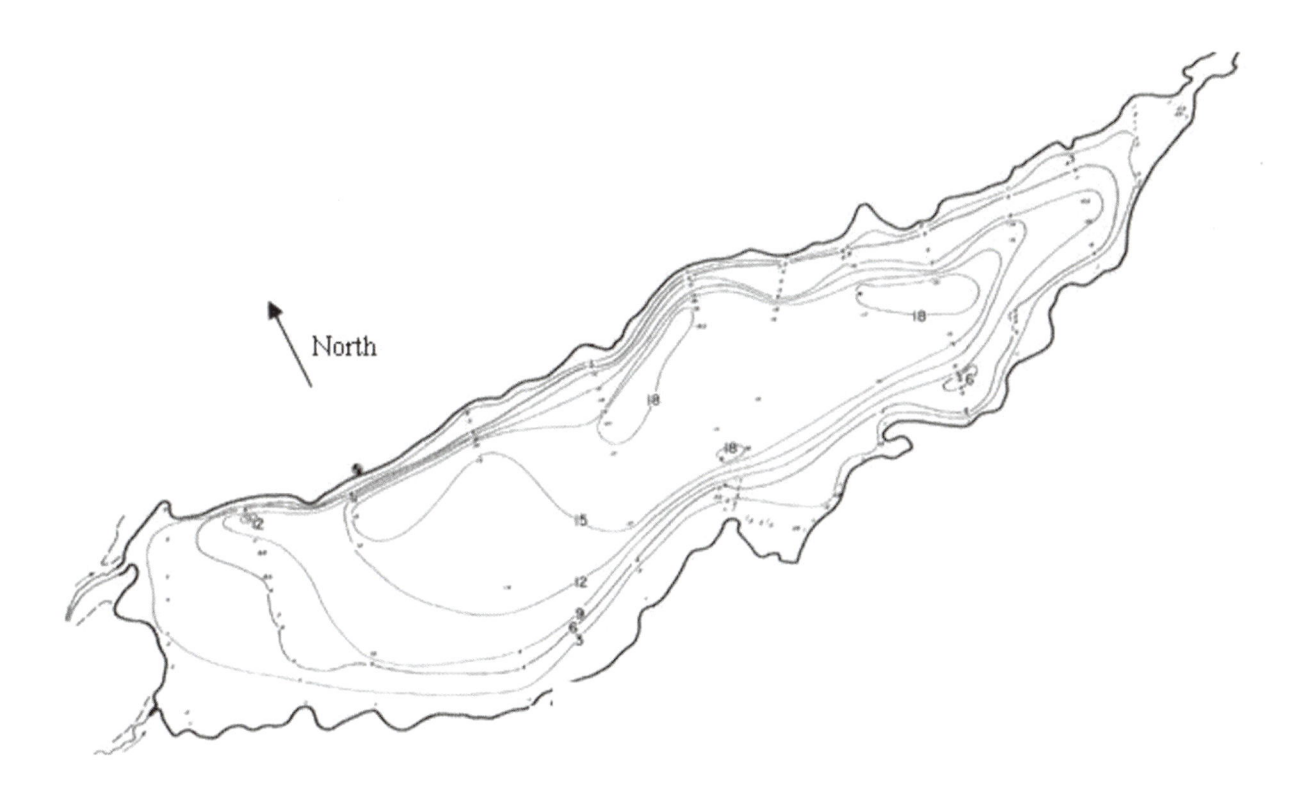

Eliguk is located on the edge of Tweedsmuir Park in the Chilcotin wilderness. It's about 350 miles north of Vancouver, about 42 miles north-northwest of Nimpo Lake, and 175 miles west of the town of Williams Lake. It is a fly-in lake using Pacific Coastal Air from Vancouver to Anaheim Lake, or by driving from Williams Lake to Nimpo Lake and then taking Tweedsmuir Air out of Nimpo Lake to Eliguk.

Gazetted name: Eliguk lake (Source: BC Ministry of Environment)

General location: In the Chilcotin 42 miles north-northwest of Nimpo Lake.

Surface area: 898 acres

Elevation: 3575 feet

Maximum depth: 68 feet

Regulations: (readers consult current issue)
  1. Daily limit: 4 trout
  2. Bait ban
  3, Single barbless hook

Photograph of Eliguk Lake taken from the lodge area.

The resort on Eliguk Lake was started in 1977 by Moe and Jeannette Schiller and is now run by Jonathan Pim (flyfishinginc@hotmail.com). It has six cabins and a lodge. They furnish all meals, boats, and motors. Fly fishing is encouraged, and that the lake is limited to single barbless hooks. Eliguk Lake is loaded with trout, and all the spawning is natural, with no plants. Eliguk Lake is quite large with lots of room for all its fly fishers; you can't miss at this lake!

Many of the popular BC trout flies are effective here, including Gils Monster, Olive Willie, Carey Specials, Wooly Buggers, Leeches, and dry flies (see the chapter "Must-have Flies"). For many years the resident expert at this lake has been Gil Nyerges, a famous northwest fly fisher. Over the past few years, another excellent fly fisher, Perry Barth from the Lynnwood, Washington area, has planned, coordinated, and guided trips to Eliguk. Perry is a member of the Olympic Fly Fishers of Edmonds as well as the Washington Fly Club of Seattle.

FAWN LAKE

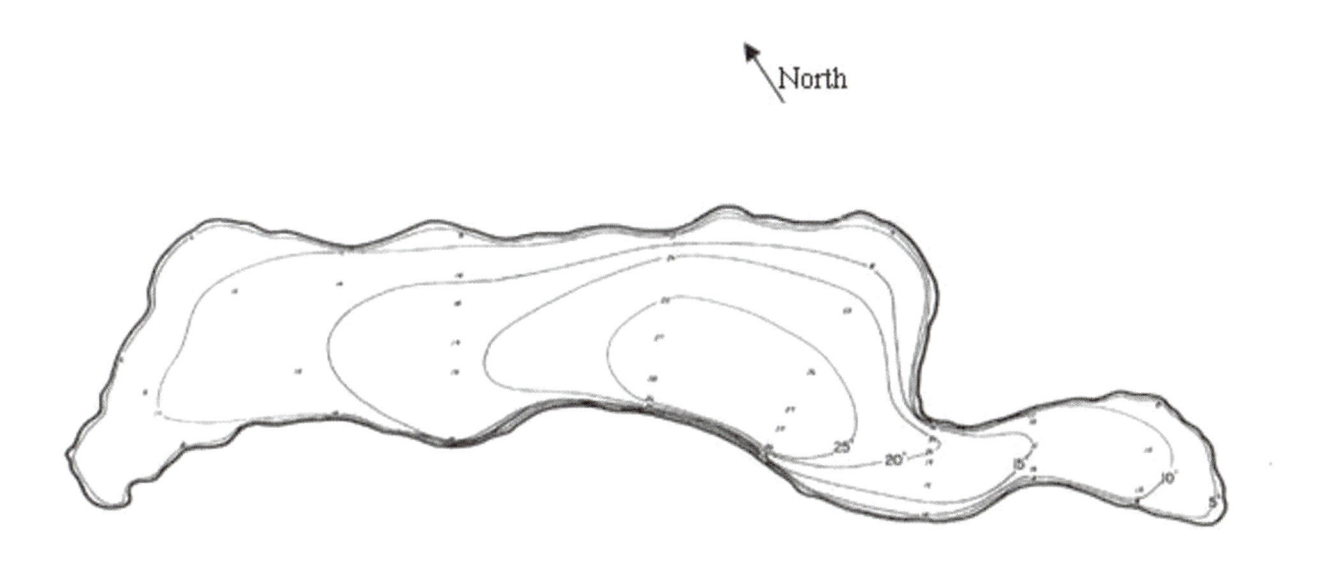

Access to Fawn Lake is gained by taking Highway 97 north from Cache Creek and then turning right onto Highway 24 (the Bridge Lake Road). Drive east about 15.5 miles, then turn left onto the Fawn Creek Road. After another 15.5 miles, turn right on a road leading to Fawn Lake. The resort at Fawn Lake offers tent sites, RV sites, and cabins. For the fly fisher, this lake offers rich insect shoals and good chironomid fishing (especially the Ice Cream Cone pattern). Leech patterns and Nymphs are also effective.

Gazetted name: Fawn Lake (Source: BC Ministry of Environment)

General Location: Southeast of the 100-Mile House on the Bridge Lake Road.

Surface area: 79.04 acres

Elevation: 3614.5 feet

Maximum depth: 28.8 feet

Regulations: (readers consult current issue)
 1. Electric motors only

Fawn Lake is stocked annually with rainbow trout from the Pennask hatchery. It is noteworthy that in 1988 and again in 1992, this lake was stocked with some of the Gerrard trout (3,000 in 1992 and 5,000 in 1988). These trout are piscivores (fish eaters) and grow rapidly. These were part of the 15,000 total trout planted each of those 2 years.

\multicolumn{3}{c}{Fawn Lake History}			
Year	Fish	Stage	Year	Fish	Stage
1952	20,000	Fry	1984	10,000	
1953	25,000	Fry	1986	5,000	
1954	18,000	Fry	1987	12,000	
1955	35,000	Fry	1988	17,000	
1956	35,000	Fry	1989	12,000	Yearlings
1957	34,995	Fry	1990	12,000	Yearlings
1958	7,000	Fry	1991	12,000	Yearlings
1959	6,000	Fingerling	1992	15,000	Yearlings
1960	12,000	Fingerling	1993	12,000	Yearlings
1961	9,000	Fingerling	1994	15,000	Yearlings
1962	12,000	Fry	1995	20,000	Yearlings
1964	8,000	Fingerling	1996	15,000	Yearlings
1967	6,500	Fry	1997	15,000	Yearlings
1970	8,000	Fingerling	1998	15,000	Yearlings
1971	5,000	Fry	1999	15,000	Yearlings
1972	8,000	Fingerling	2000	15,000	Yearlings
1973	2,000	Fry	2001	15,000	Yearlings
1974	13,900	Fingerling	2002	15,000	Yearlings
1979	7,500		2003	15,000	Yearlings
1980	10,000		2004	15,000	Yearlings
1981	10,000		2005	15,000	Yearlings
1982	10,000		2006	15,000	Yearlings
1983	7,500		2007	15,000	Yearlings
			2008	15,000	Yearlings
			2009	15,000	Yearlings

GLIMPSE LAKE

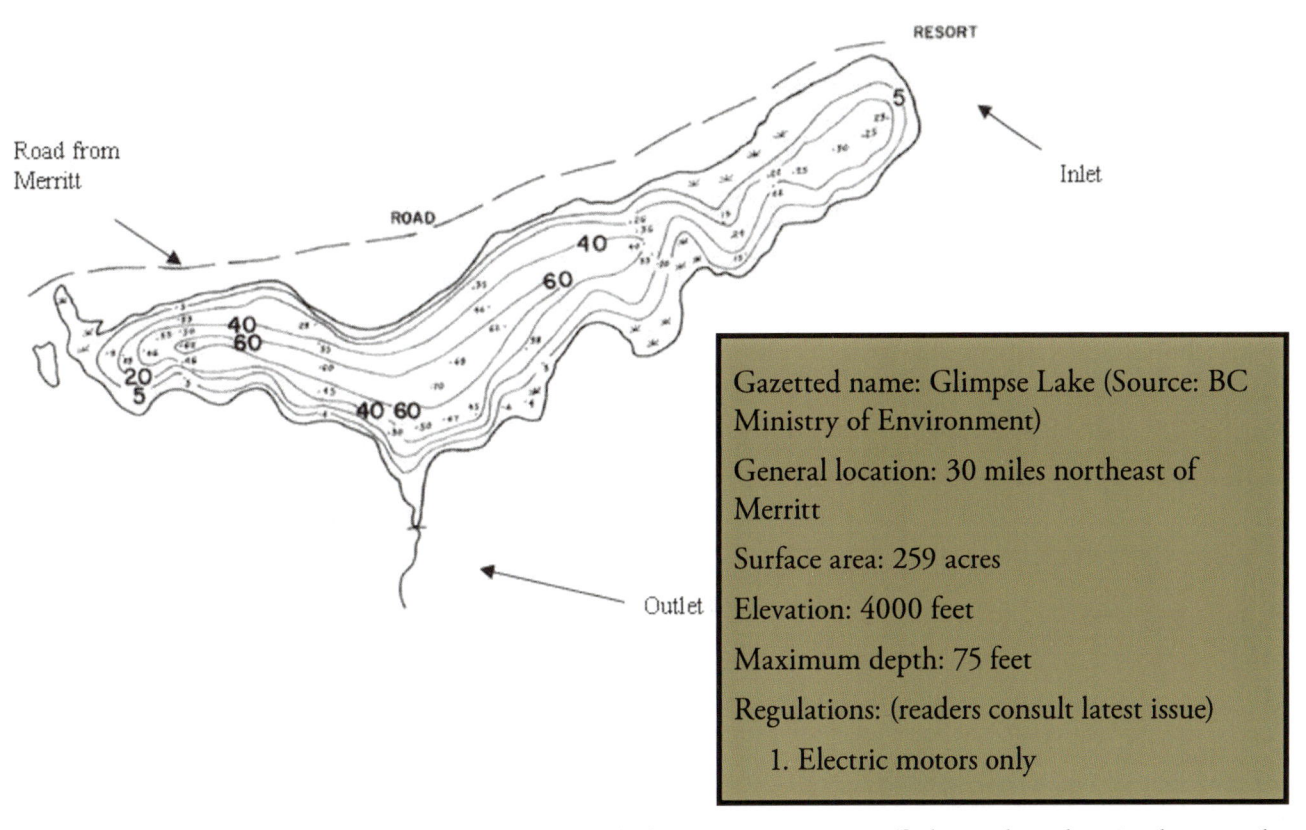

Gazetted name: Glimpse Lake (Source: BC Ministry of Environment)

General location: 30 miles northeast of Merritt

Surface area: 259 acres

Elevation: 4000 feet

Maximum depth: 75 feet

Regulations: (readers consult latest issue)
 1. Electric motors only

To find Glimpse Lake, take Highway 5A north from Merritt, turn off alongside Lake Nicola onto the Douglas Lake Road, and then turn left onto Lauder Road. It's about eight miles up to the lake.

Good hatches occur of chironomids, damsels, and sedges and occasionally a Water Boatman hatch in the fall. Popular flies to use include Tom Thumb, Wooly Bugger, Ice Cream Cone, Mike Shellito's gray chironomid, Nyerges Nymph, Shrimp, Black O'Lindsay, Grizzly King, and Leeches.

The best fishing is when the hatches occur in May and June and again in the fall in September and October, before the turnover begins or after it is finished.

A PERSONAL HISTORY OF GLIMPSE LAKE

My original introduction to Glimpse Lake came by way of my high school

Kevin Gould (when a bit younger) with fish from Glimpse Lake

neighbor and early fishing partner, Jim Swift, who lived near me in Seattle. Jim and his folks began fishing Glimpse Lake back in the '40s and '50s when the lake was an outstanding fishery. Jim called me over to his home one day in 1950 and showed me a refrigerator full of lovely trout from Glimpse Lake—and to top it off he showed me one more trout too large to go into the refrigerator because it weighed eleven pounds. More stories about the big fish eventually led to my first trip to Glimpse Lake in September 1958 with my sister, Barbara; her husband, Wilbur Watson; and my wife, Susan.

Originally Glimpse Lake was known as Silver Lake, then Hawkins Lake, and finally Glimpse Lake. The lodge was built in 1916 by W. Hawkins. Bob and Helen Albrecht bought the property in 1927 and began a fox farm that was unsuccessful; they later changed it to a fishing resort.

Our annual trips to Glimpse Lake resulted is fast friendships with Bob, Helen, and their hired hand, George. Bob regaled us with many stories, including how the lake was barren of fish when he arrived there; he claimed he undertook the task of planting the lake by riding horseback to Pennask Lake and bringing back trout in saddle bags. No sign of those fish he planted occurred until three years later when he found an eleven-pound trout in the spawning stream next to the lodge. Interesting enough, the BC government's records confirm that Glimpse Lake was originally stocked with ten thousand Pennask rainbow eggs in 1929, and it has been planted every year since. Reports of huge trout were confirmed by net samplings taken by BC fisheries in 1950–1952. They showed fish as large as nine to eleven pounds. By 1995 the big fish story had completely changed. Netting surveys by Brian Chan's folks then showed the average fish was between eleven and twelve inches long, with the largest weighing three pounds.

During our early trips to Glimpse Lake, we stayed in cabin A and cabin B near the lodge. Later on in 1961, we discovered another old logger's cabin about a mile down the lake from the lodge and asked to stay there; we have done so every year since. It was designated as cabin F. Bob was aghast that we'd want to stay in such a primitive place, but we persisted. He finally arranged to have the roof repaired and had a porch added to the cabin. An event that occurred during one of our trips to Glimpse in the late 1950s caused me to become a fly fisherman forever. I can still recall magic evening when I landed an eighteen-inch beauty at dusk on a floating line using a Black O'Lindsay. That experience made me a real believer in fly fishing and made me realize how much fun it was.

Glimpse Lake has a way of working its special magic on those who fish there. My sister Barbara had become particularly close to Bob and Helen Albrecht and worked one summer in the lodge helping out. She captured the pure essence of that magic in a poem she wrote in 1966 titled "Sing a Song of Glimpse Lake."

Sing a song of Glimpse Lake

A pocket full of flies
Four and twenty flatfish
Will surely bring a rise.
When the smokehouse opens
George begins to sing,
Isn't that a dainty dish
Fit for any king?
The dogs are in a meadow
Routing out a quail
While Sue weeps o'er a Kamloops
That hasn't any tail
Wil is up in Story's end
Doing mighty fine
When along comes an osprey
And snips off his line!
Ray has hooked a lunker
He knows the prize will take
But the fish leaps out the trusty net
And swims away up lake.
Barbara's on the near bank
Basking in the sun
When along comes a black bear
And puts her on the run!
Bob is in the pump house
Wrestling with some gear
And Helen stalks a mushroom
In a woodland spot quite near.
With Solunar Table guidance
We fish the fading light
And listen as the loons cry
And call out in the night.
The cattle trail away
And we hurry off to Cabin F
To plot another day.

-The cast of characters mentioned in this poem, in the order in which they appear, are as follows: "George" was Albrecht's handyman, "Sue" was Sue Gould, "Wil" was Wilbur Watson, "Ray" was Ray Gould, "Barbara" was Barbara Watson, "Bob" was Bob Albrecht, and "Helen" was Helen Albrecht.

As time marched on, changes became inevitable. Helen Albrecht died in 1970 and is buried near a large tree next to the lodge. Bob moved to a small trailer alongside Nicola Lake for a short time, and he later moved to his homeland Switzerland to be near his sister Gabrielle, who lived in Geneva.

Sadly the inexorable pressure for development took place. Albrecht sold the lodge to a developer, who in turn leased the property to Bruce Grant. Bruce operated the lodge for about ten years. I got to know Bruce Grant quite well and told him that if the property was ever sold, I would be interested in buying cabin F. Meanwhile the developer arranged for fifty-six lots to be sold off along the north side of the lake. And so it came to pass that on June 30, 1976, I bought cabin F. In 1981 the developer then sold the lodge and property to a party named John Grain and Terra7. Eventually Grain sold the property to Alex Schuetz, who formed the Little Beaver Creek Ranch. He in turn is selling off seven more sites along the north shore of the lake. During all of these years, development resulted in logging along the spawning creek, damming of the creek by beavers, and intense human pressures on the lake. Yet one side of the lake remains in a natural state, reminding us of the beauty that once was.

Ray Gould

One interesting thing that has been done by us fly fishers in cabin F each year was to keep a log called a "troutography." It is a record sheet posted inside the cabin door of cabin F each year whereby each fisherman is asked to record the length of each trout landed. A summary of this data is sent each year to Brian Chan, Steve Maricle, and now to Ken Scheer of the Fresh Water Fishing Society of BC, who now schedule the planting of the lakes. They have records of the planting of Glimpse Lake back to 1929, and they have my troutography summaries and graphs since 1958 to assist them in having data to support their plans.

My data shows a fairly constant length of fish between the years of 1972–1996, with an average of about thirteen inches. Then in 1996 the number of planted trout was steadily cut from fifteen thousand yearlings down to only five thousand yearlings in 2004, resulting in a much lower number of fish caught but a gradual increase in the size. I asked the BC fisheries people to return the plant to fifteen thousand yearlings, and they agreed to do so. They planted twelve thousand yearlings in 2005, then fifteen thousand in 2006–2009.

glimpse lake History

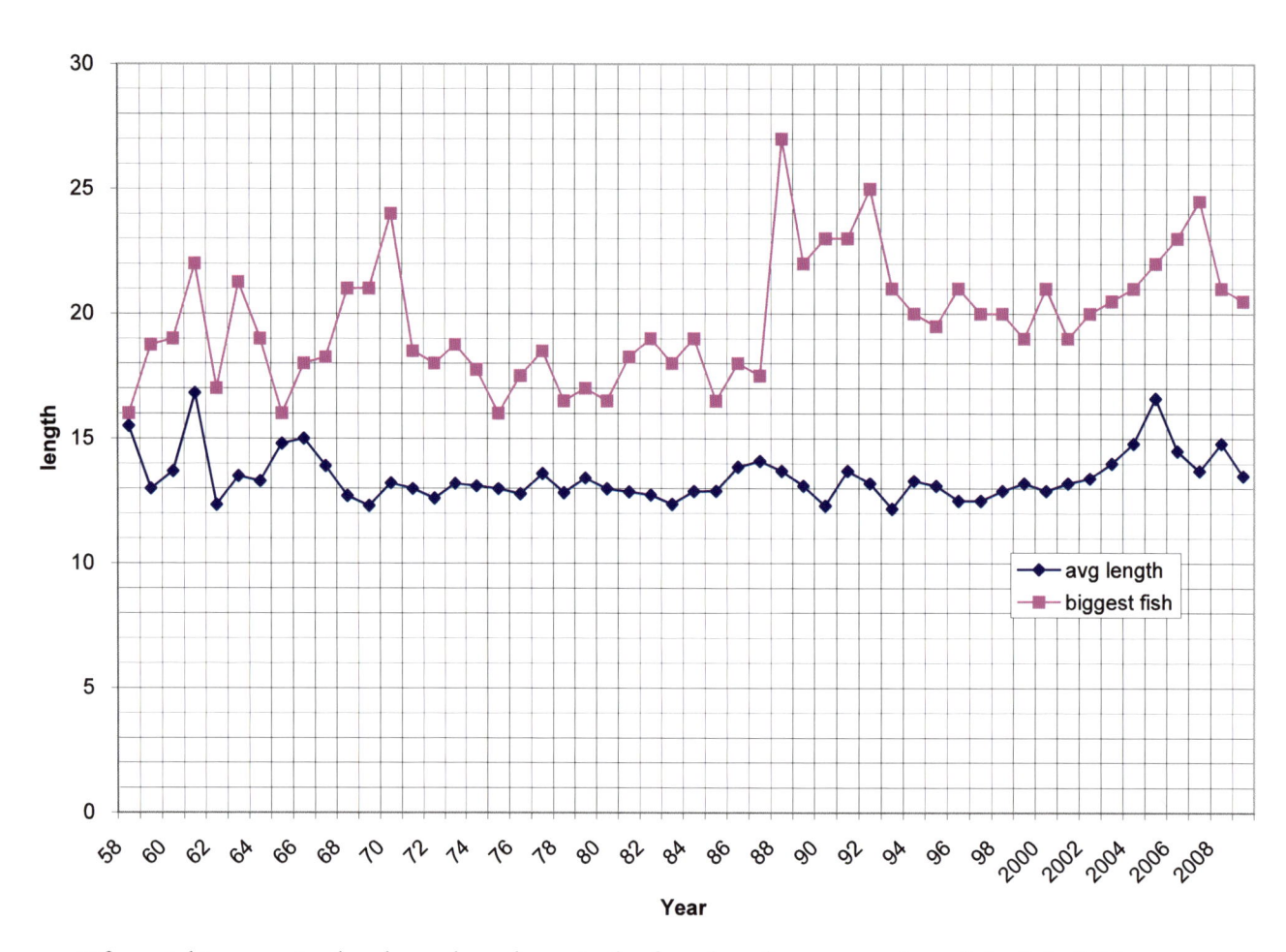

Of special interest in the above data charts is the fact that the average size of the fish did increase each year from 2000–2006, resulting from the decreased plant during those years. But the number of fish taken during those years fell precipitously, so fly fishers lost interest. Part of this condition was due to the fact that several low-water years occurred during that time, resulting in little, if any, natural recruitment. The trick is to find a balance so that there is plenty of action but some larger fish are available. See the following graph showing the number of fish planted in Glimpse Lake each year.

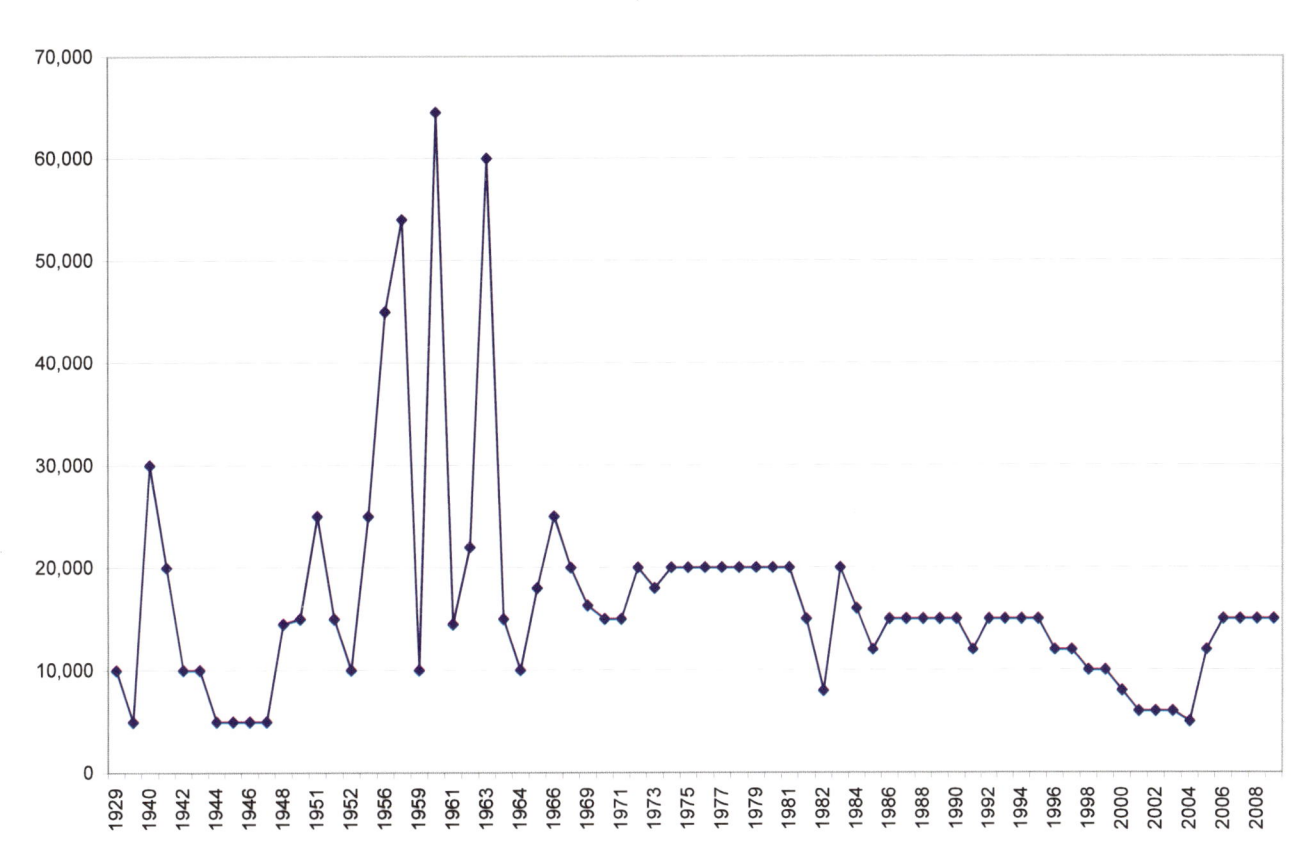

The dock at cabin F, looking toward the "pocket" end of the lake

Hatheume Lake

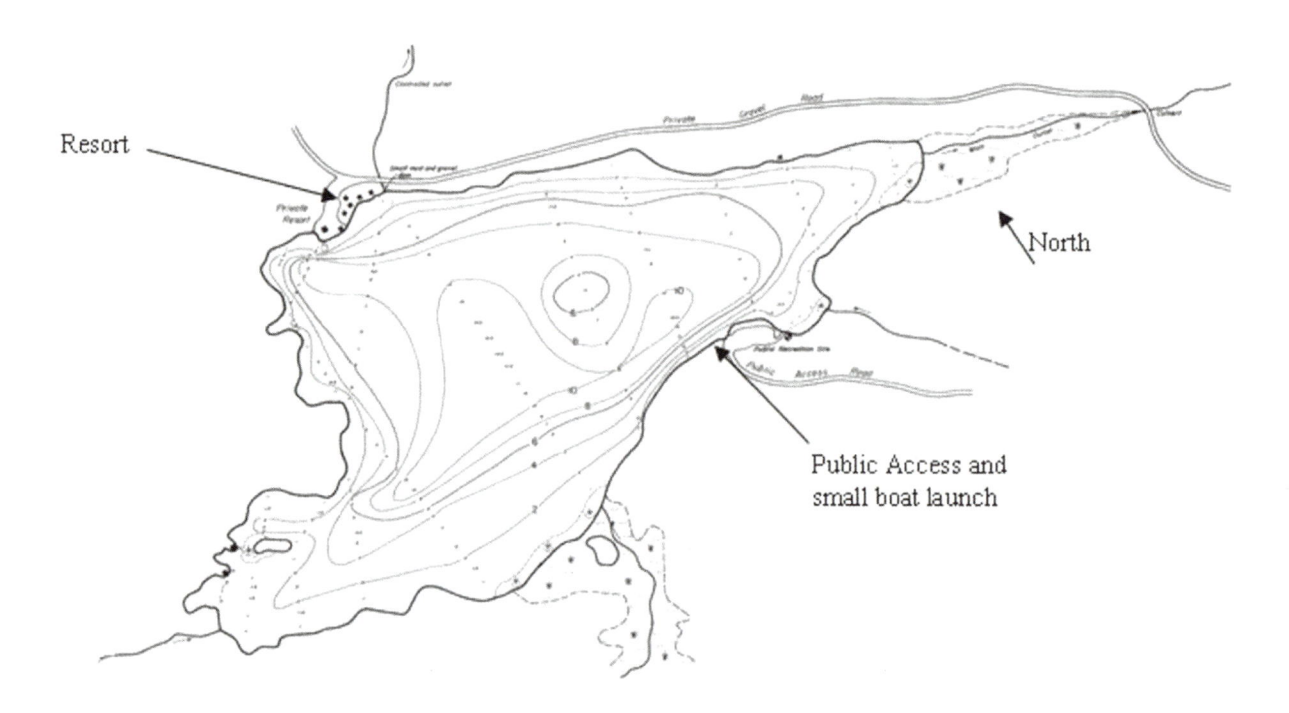

Hatheume is located about fifty miles east of Merritt close to Pennask Lake. It can be reached via highway 97C. Leave this Okanogan connector at the Sunset exit, take the Sunset Lake Forest Service Road, and then take the Bear Creek Forest Service Road.

There is a nice campground located on the southeast end of the lake.

Because the lake is planted with some triploid trout, it produces some nice sized fish. In earlier years it contained very large shrimp, providing a rich diet for the fish. Popular fly patterns here are chironomids, sedges, damsels, and dragonflies. The first time I fished this lake was in 1964. Although I only landed three fish they weighed 4 pounds, five pounds and 6 pounds respectively.

The resort on the northwest corner of the lake was originally run by the Redstone family, then by Tullis and Avery of Everett. This resort is being sold to private owners via Triple 8 Development.

Gazetted name: Hatheume lake (Source: BC Ministry of Environment)

General location: 50 miles east of Merritt

Surface area: 261 acres

Elevation: 3576 feet

Maximum depth: 40 feet

Regulations: (readers consult latest issue)

1. Closed to fishing December 1 through April 30
2. Daily limit: 1 fish
3. Artificial flies only, single barbless hook, bait ban
4. Engine power restricted to 10 HP.

Please see the following chart for the stocking history of Hatheume Lake. Note that the plant has been reduced from 3,500 to 2,000 in 2009 as compared to previous years, and that this plant is all yearlings.

Hatheume Lake Stocking History						
Year	Diploid	Stage	Year	Diploid	Triploid	Stage
1928	8,000	Egg	1986	2,000		Yearling
1936	40,000	Fry	1987	9,200		Yearling
1945	10,000	Fry	1988	5,090		Yearling
1958	15,000	Fingerling	1989	4,500		Yearling
1959	10,000	Fingerling	1990	3,346		Yearling
1960	18,000	Fingerling	1991	1,000		Yearling
1961	20,000	Fry	1992	1,000		Yearling
1962	31,000	Fry	1993	3,000		Yearling
1963	50,000	Yearling	1994	1,000		Yearling
1966	70,000	Fry	1995	2,000		Yearling
1967	40,000	Fry	1996	2,000		Yearling
1968	70,000	Fry	1997	2,000		Yearling
1969	70,000	Fry	1998	2,000	1,500	Yrlg/Fingrl
1970	70,000	Fry	1999	2,000	1,500	Yrlg/Fingrl
1971	50,000	Fry	2000	2,000	1500	Yrlg/Fingrl
1973	50,000	Fry	2001		3,500	Yrlg/Fingrl
1974	30,000	Fingerling	2002		3,500	Yrlg/Fingrl
1975	30,000	Fingerling	2003		3,500	Yrlg/Fingrl
1982	13,800	Yearling	2004		3,500	Yrlg/Fingrl
1983	12,000	Yearling	2005		3,500	Yrlg/Fingrl
1984	15,000	Yearling	2006		3,500	Yrlg/Fingrl
1985	23,800	Yearling	2007		3,500	Yrlg/Fingrl
			2008		3,500	Yrlg/Fingrl
			2009		2,000	Yearling

HiHium Lake

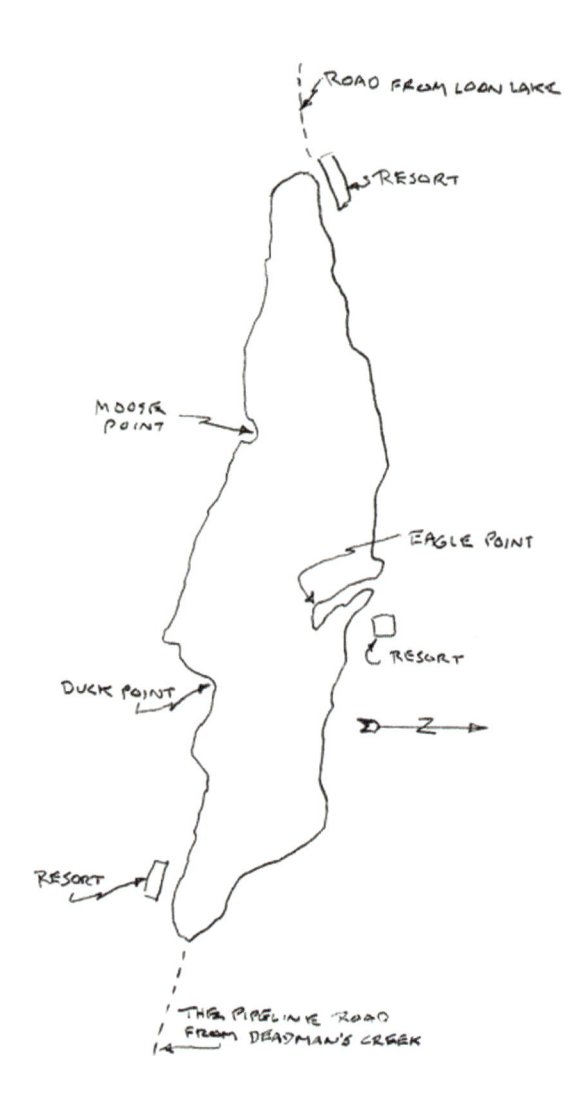

> Gazetted name: HiHium (Source: BC Ministry of Environment)
>
> General location: East of Clinton
>
> Surface area: 865 acres
>
> Elevation: 4485 feet
>
> Maximum depth: 23 feet
>
> Regulations: (readers consult latest issue)
>
>   1. Daily limit: 2 fish
>   2. Single barbless hook
>   3. Closed to fishing December 1 through April 30
>   4. Engine power restricted to 10 HP

HiHium is a lake long favored by many anglers. It is situated east of the town of Clinton and can be reached in a couple ways, including a road from the south end of Loon Lake. This road leads to Ladoski's Resort on the west end of the lake. There also is a campground on the east end of the lake, which in days gone by could be reached by going up the old pipe line road from Deadman's Creek. Two other resorts on the lake are the Circle W and the Sky High facilities.

HiHium, which means "mother of all fish," is a large lake about four miles long, but it is relatively shallow with a maximum depth of twenty-three feet. It's best to have a stable boat with an outboard motor for fishing this lake. During the warm summer months the lake gets a fairly heavy bloom, but fishing is good in the spring and again in the fall.

Known for its sedge hatches and shrimp populations, the lake often produces good fly fishing. I have fished this lake three times and took fish up to twenty-three inches on each trip.

One note of caution: the taste of the fish seems to be a bit muddy, but this may be due to the particular time of year.

See the following chart for the planting information.

HiHium Lake Fish Stocking History					
Year	Diploids	Size	Year	Diploids	Size
1973	25,000	Fry	1990	30,000	Fall Fry
1974	40,000	Fry	1991	30,000	Fall Fry
1975	40,000	Fry	1992	30,000	Fry
1976	40,000		1993	30,000	Fry
1978	55,000		1994	30,000	Fall Fry
1979	40,000		1995	31,000	Fall Fry
1980	40,000		1996	25,000	Fall Fry
1981	40,000		1997	25,000	Fall Fry
1982	40,000		1998	25,000	Fall Fry
1983	40,000		1999	48,825	Fall Fry
1984	40,000		2000	25,000	Fall Fry
1985	40,000		2001	25,000	Fall Fry
1986	40,000		2002	20,000	Fall Fry
1987	40,000		2003	15,000	Fall Fry
1988	40,000		2004	20,000	Fall Fry
1989	40,000	Fall Fry	2005	20,000	Fry
			2006	20,000	Fall Fry
			2007	20,000	Fry
			2008	20,356	Fry
			2009	20,000	Fry

BIG OK (ISLAND) LAKE

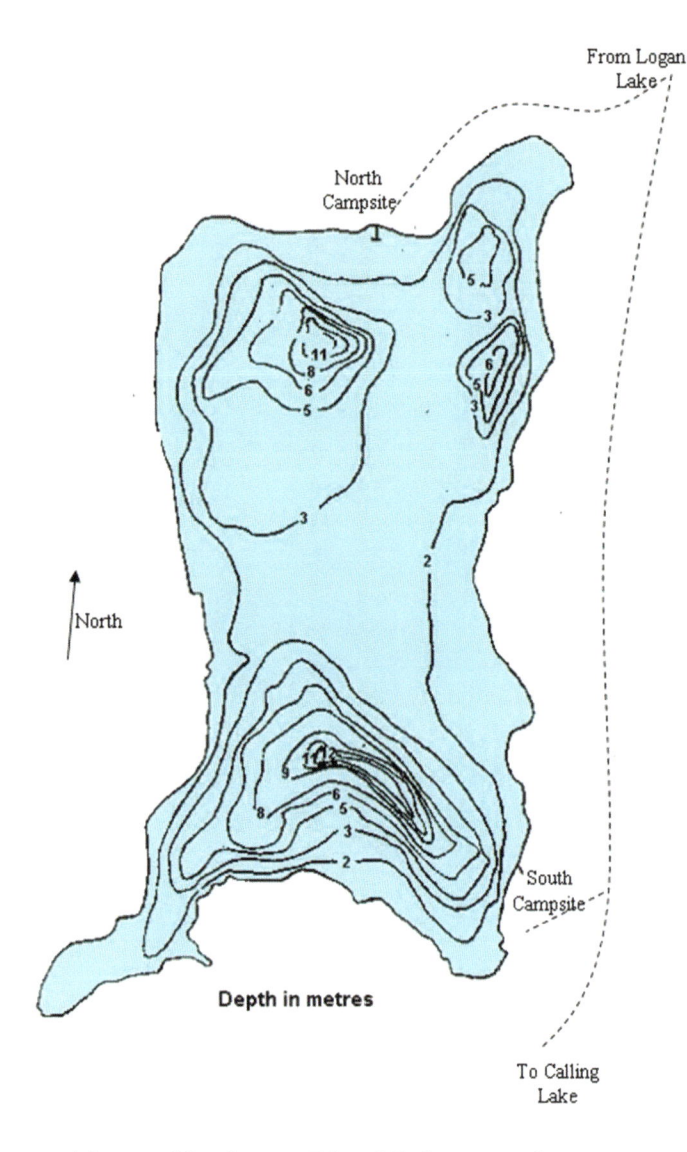

Gazetted name: Big OK (Island) Lake (Source: BC Adventure.com and BC Ministry of Environment)

General location: West of Logan Lake

Surface Area: 84 acres

Elevation: 5000 feet

Maximum depth: 40 feet

Regulations: (readers consult latest issue)
1. Closed to fishing December 1 through April 30
2. Rainbow Trout release
3. Artificial fly only, bait ban
4. Single barbless hook
5. Engine power restricted to 10 HP

The road leading to Island Lake is tough to navigate but the trip is certainly worth the effort. It's best to have a truck or SUV for this trip. To get there, take 97C west from the town of Logan Lake. As you travel west, you'll go past the Highland Valley Copper Mine and then past its tailings pond. Turn left onto the Laura Lake Road; at this point the road is no longer paved and passes through mine property going just behind the huge dam at the end of the tailings pond. After passing the dam the road is no longer maintained and is full of chuck holes and mud holes. The road is signed, so pay attention to them. After traveling some twelve to thirteen miles, the road passes along the east side of Island Lake. There are two accesses to the lake, one on the north end and one on the south end. Note that this road eventually leads to Calling Lake one mile farther.

The launching area on the south end is steep and difficult but close to the good fishing areas on the lake. The camping and launching area on the north end is larger but not easy to get to.

Photo of Big OK taken from south end; the light spot in foreground is the underwater island

The name Big OK (Island) Lake sometimes causes confusion because there are at least three island lakes in British Columbia. Somehow this one also got dubbed "Big OK" to differentiate it from the others. The lake has the special feature of a big underwater island in the middle of the lake and some deep water at either end. There is no resort, and neither are there any cabins or facilities at this lake. Thus it's either day fishing or rough camping.

Big OK (Island) Lake is situated at the five-thousand-foot elevation and is fairly small, being only about eighty-four acres in size. It's a very pretty lake surrounded by forests. Be careful on the trip because there has been much logging in the area in recent years.

A good way to fish the lake is to anchor on the shoal on the edge of the island and cast out to deeper water using a chironomid or shrimp fly. When the sedge fly hatch is on in the spring, the caddis fly patterns such as the Tom Thumb or the Black O'Lindsay are also effective.

One of the conditions that make this lake attractive is its remoteness. Another is that it produces large trout. This can be traced to several factors, including being planted with triploids most every year since 1991. The number of fish planted has been relatively small at only twenty-three fish per acre, but in 2009 the plant quantity was increased to three thousand yearlings, making the density thirty-five fish per acre. Even so, anglers have to work for their catches. See the following table.

Big OK Lake (Island) Fish Stocking History					
Year					
	Diploids	Triploids	All Female	Size	
1976	5,000				
1977	5,000				
1978	5,000				
1979	5,000				
1981	5,000				
1983	5,000				
1984	5,000				
1985	7,000				
1986	5,000				
1987	7,000				
1988	5,000				
1989	4,000			Fall Fry	
1990	3,000			Fall Fry	
1991	800	800	800	Yearling	
1992	1,500			Yearling	
1993	1,235	500	500	Yearling	
1994		1,060	190	Yearling	
1995		500		Yearling	
1996	1,059		477	Yearling	
1998		2,010	250	Yearling	
1999		2767		Fingerling	
2000		2,774		Yearling	
2001		2770		Yrlg/Fgrlg	
2002		2,750		Yrlg/Fgrlg	
2003		3,000		Yrlg/Fgrlg	
2004		3,144		Yrlg/Fgrlg	
2005		3,000		Yrlg/Fgrlg	
2006		2,000		Yrlg/Fgrlg	
2007		2,000		Yearling	
2008		2,000		Yearling	
2009		3,000		Yearling	

JANICE LAKE

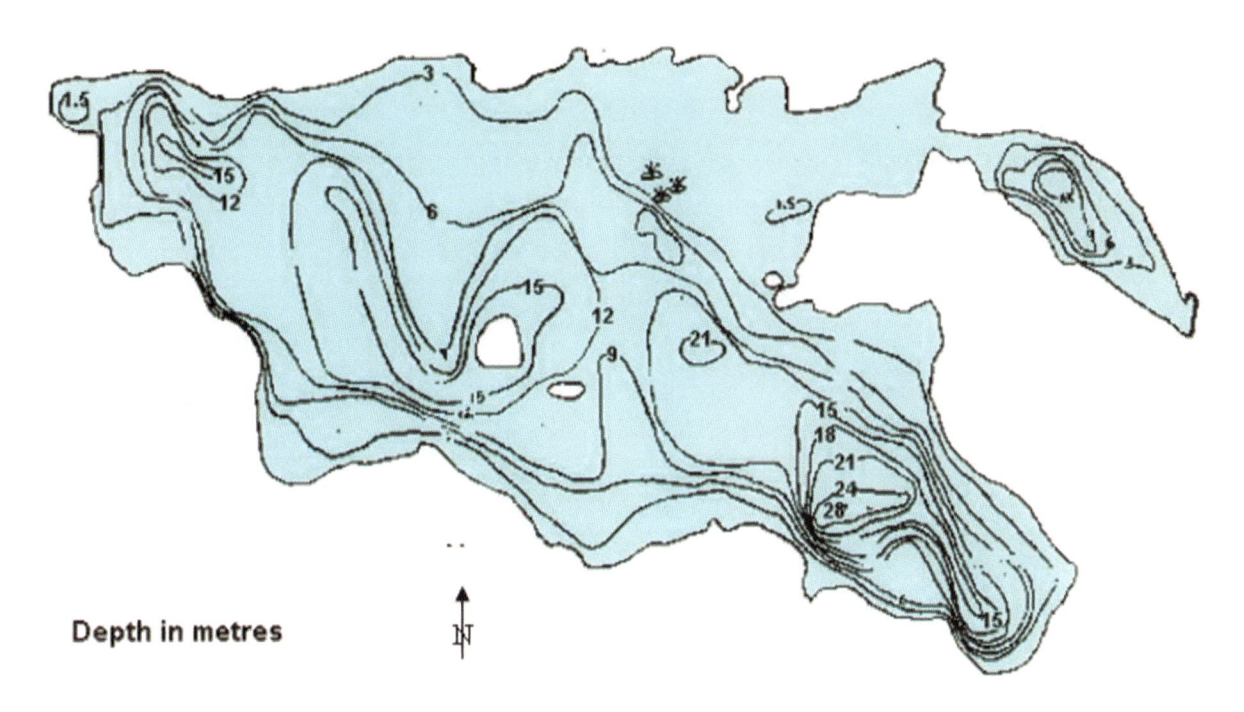

Depth in metres

To find Janice Lake, take Hwy 5 north out of Kamloops and then take the Bridge Lake Road (Hwy 24) west from Little Fort. Travel about fourteen miles and take the turn off to the left to Long Island Lake (Janice Lake). It is a lovely lake and has very good fly fishing. The resort on the lake is operated by Bob and Silver Cartwright have operated the resort for many years. If you haven't had pancakes made by Silver Cartwright, you haven't lived! Silver tells an interesting story about how she was named. It seems her father was a professional gambler who spent some considerable time in this endeavor. When he returned one evening from a very successful outing, he learned that, in his absence, he had become the father of a baby daughter. He was so pleased with these events that he named his new daughter "Silver." A true story? Only Silver knows for sure!

Besides the resort there is also a forest service campground located at the northeast corner of the lake. Janice Lake was originally stocked in 1956 and 1957 with eighteen thousand rainbow trout in each of those two years. There is no evidence of fisheries having stocked it since then; natural recruitment sustains the lake. Fly fishing is usually good in the spring and fall with strong hatches of sedges and chironomids. Another pattern that has been particularly successful here is the Water Cricket. See the instructions for

Gazetted name: Long Island Lake; alias Janice Lake (Source: BC Ministry of Environment and BC Adventure.com)

General location: Northwest of Little Fort

Surface Area: 362 acres

Elevation: 4166 feet

Maximum depth: 91 feet

Regulations: (readers consult latest issue)

1. Closed to fishing December 1 through April 30

tying this pattern in the chapter "Must Have Flies." The contours of the lake provide good shoals and drop-offs for anchoring and casting.

A new acquaintance of mine, Belle Marie Rightmire, also has enjoyed fishing at Janice Lake. She and her husband found it to be a lovely spot resulting in a memorable fishing experience. Belle's brother-in-law, Gordon Rightmire, was a regular at Janice for some ten to fifteen years. He and his buddies usually fished the lake during the end of June and took many fish in the twelve to fourteen inch range, with a few larger ones up to two pounds. His favorite flies included the Muddler Minnow and the sedge fly. Gordon confirms that to his knowledge the lake is not planted but relies on natural production.

Janice Lake viewed from the lodge
Photo by Curtiss Rightmire

LAC LE JEUNE

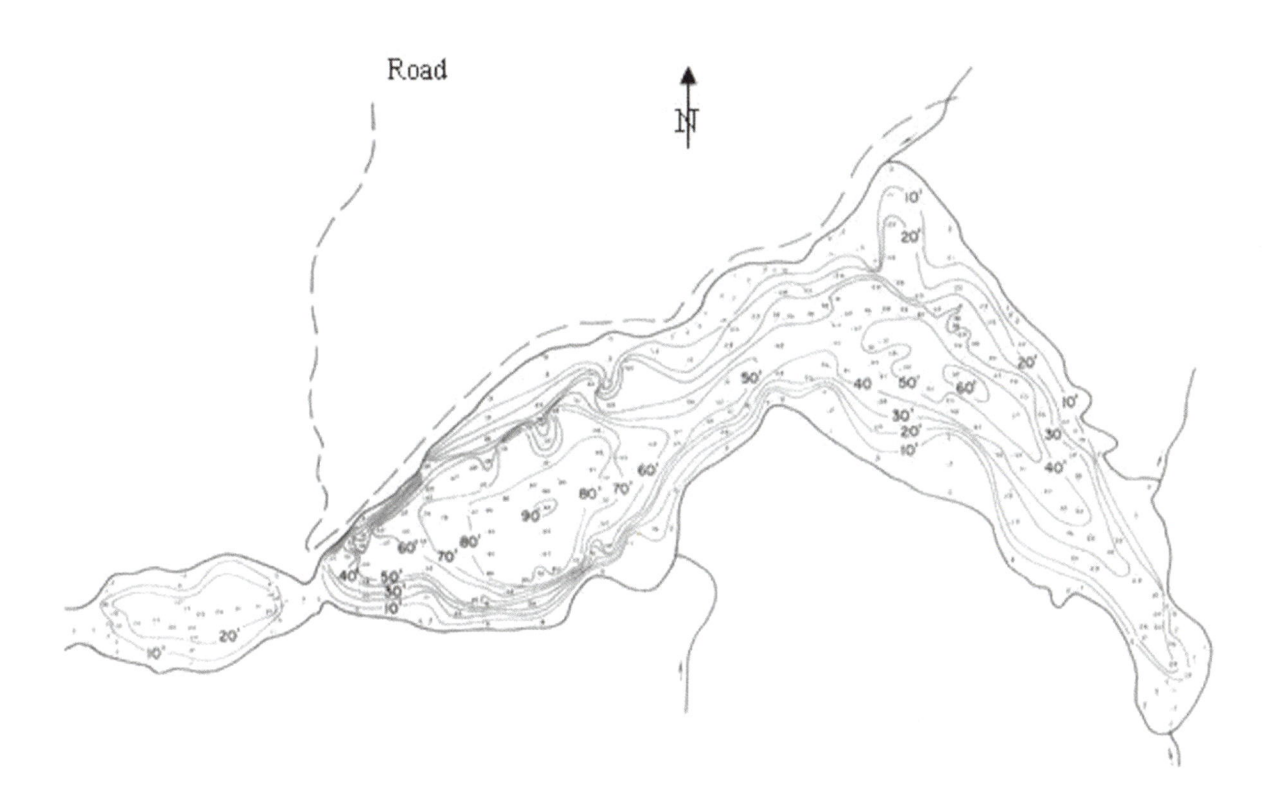

If there ever was a well-known, famous, storied lake in British Columbia, it is Lac Le Jeune. This 393-acre gem is situated at an elevation of a bit over 4,000 feet and is located 22 miles south of the city of Kamloops just west of the Coquihalla highway.

What has made this lake so special is that it was originally stocked in 1923 and in the 1930s received many plants of 250,000 fish. Thus many fish were available and made it a popular spot. From 1995–2009 the fish plant each year has held steady at the much lower level of 15,000 yearlings. This may be caused by the fact that Lac Le Jeune is used more as a family lake and for camping and relaxing outings, with its two resorts and provincial campsite.

Gazetted name: Lac Le Jeune (Source: BC Ministry of Environment)

General location: South of Kamloops

Surface area: 393 acres

Elevation: 4000 feet

Maximum depth: 88 feet

Regulations: (readers consult latest issue)
  1. Speed restriction: 20 km/hr

For a summary of the fish stocking history, please see the following chart.

Lac Le Jeune Lake Stocking History

Year	Diploids	Stage	Year	Diploids	Stage
1923	30,000	Eggs	1977	30,000	
1931	267,000	Fry	1978	30,000	
1932	253,925	Fry	1979	30,000	
1933	257,000	Fry	1980	30,000	
1934	250,000	Fry	1981	25,000	
1935	250,000	Fry	1982	30,000	
1936	250,000	Fry	1983	35,000	
1937	250,000	Fry	1984	25,000	
1938	100,000	Fry	1985	17,800	
1939	100,000	Fry	1986	25,000	
1940	100,000	Fry	1987	25,000	
1941	100,000	Fry	1988	15,000	
1946	75,000	Fry/Eggs	1989	25,000	Yearling
1947	100,000	Fry	1990	25,000	Yearling
1949	80,000	Fry	1991	25,000	Yearling
1950	50,000	Fry	1992	31,000	Yearling
1951	50,000	Fry	1993	25,000	Yearling
1952	80,000	Fry	1994	25,079	Yearling
1953	80,000	Fry	1995	15,000	Yearling
1954	90,000	Fry	1996	15,000	Yearling
1956	63,500	Fry	1997	15,000	Yearling
1962	70,000	Fry	1998	15,000	Yearling
1963	70,000	Fry	1999	15,000	Yearling
1968	150,000	Fry	2000	15,999	Yearling
1969	102,000	Fingerling	2001	15,000	Yearling
1970	25,000	Fingerling	2002	15,000	Yearling
1971	35,000	Fry	2003	15,000	Yearling
1972	50,000	Fingerling	2004	15,000	Yearling
1973	26,000	Fingerling	2005	15,000	Yearling
1974	51,000	Fingerling	2006	15,000	Yearling
1975	30,000	Fingerling	2007	15,000	Yearling
1976	30,000		2008	15,000	Yearling
			2009	15,000	Yearling

Lundbom Lake

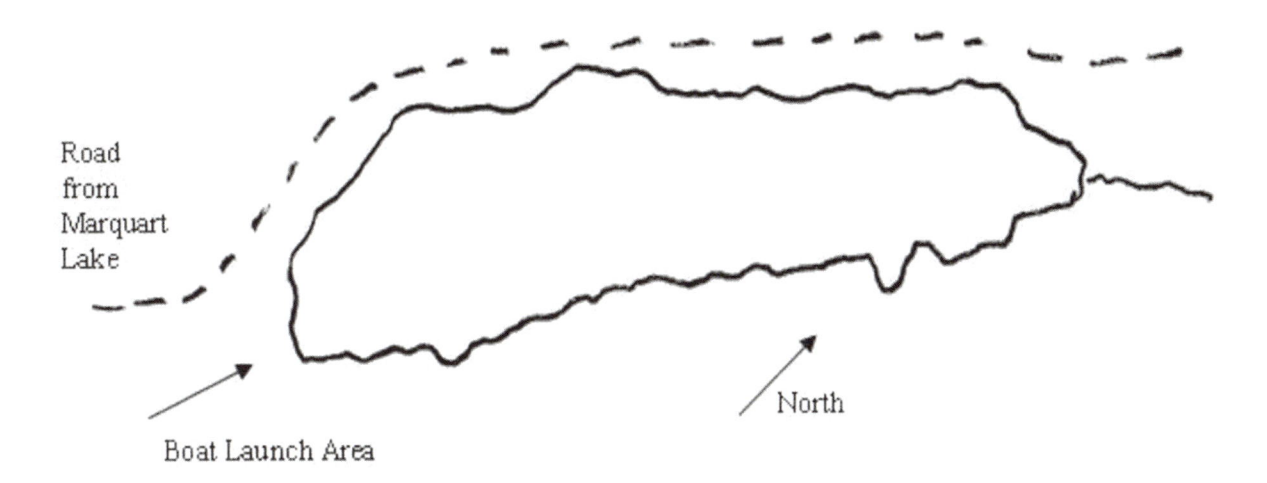

Lundbom Lake is located about nine miles east of the town of Merritt off of Highway 97C (the Coquihalla Connector). The lake is only about one mile past (East) Marquart Lake. This lake is heavily used and is under much pressure from local anglers. It has, for many years, been a favorite because it produced very large fish. Like Marquart Lake, it is best to avoid going to Lundbom Lake on a weekend or a holiday.

Gazetted name: Lundbom (data source: BC Ministry of Environment)

General location: East of Merritt

Surface area: 114 acres

Elevation: 3700 feet

Regulations: (readers consult latest issue)
 1. Closed to fishing December 1 through April 30
 2. Daily limit: 2 trout
 3. Bait ban, single barbless hook

In recent times, fish in the four- to five-pound range can be caught. This is due, in some large measure, to the planting of triploids, which has been the practice beginning in 2002. Good success can be anticipated using Tom Thumb or Black O'Lindsay flies when the caddis hatch is on, and Wooly Buggers, Dr. Spratley, or damsel nymphs at other times. See the following chart for a summary of the stocking history of this lake. Note that in 2009 one-third of the plant was of catchable size.

Lundbom Lake Fish Planting History							
Year	Diploids	Triploids	Stage	Year	Diploids	Triploids	Stage
1961	12,000		Fry	1984	12,000		
1962	12,000		Fry	1985	12,000		
1963	12,000		Fry	1986	8,000		
1964	20,000		Fry	1987	12,000		Yearling
1966	10,000		Fry	1988	10,000		
1968	6,000		Fingerling	1989	12,000		Yearling
1969	8,000		Fingerling	1990	12,000		Yearling
1970	8,000		Fingerling	1991	12,000		Yearling
1972	8,000		Fingerling	1992	8,000		Yearling
1973	7,200		Yearling	1993	12,000		Yearling
1974	8,000		Fingerling	1994	8,000		Yearling
1975	4,000		Fingerling	1995	8,000		Yearling
1976	8,000			1996	8,000		Yearling
1977	8,000			1997	8,000		Yearling
1978	10,000			1998	8,000		Yearling
1979	10,000			1999	8,000		Yearling
1980	15,000			2000	8,000		Yearling
1981	15,000			2001	8,000		Yearling
1982	15,000			2002		8,000	Yearling
1983	15,000			2003		8,000	Yearling
				2004		6,000	Yearling
				2005		6,000	Yearling
				2006		6,000	Yearling
				2007		6,000	Yearling
				2008		14,000	Yearling
				2009		9,013	Yearling

Marquart Lake

Marquart Lake is located about eight miles south of the town of Merritt off Highway 5A. There is a forest service campground and boat launch at the lake. Because this lake is so close to Merritt, it has become very popular and fishing pressure is intense. The best plans are to avoid weekends and holidays. This place is busy not only for fly fishing but for horseback riding as well.

An unusual feature of Marquart Lake is that it is one of about ten lakes in the region stocked with mixed rainbow trout and eastern brook trout. For the most part this practice has created a better fishery, but it is limited to highly productive lakes. The growth rate of both species is somewhat compromised. In the years 1997–2008, Marquart Lake has been stocked with triploids, the fast-growing trout. Note too that during those twelve years triploids were stocked, both as rainbow trout and brook trout. For a small lake it is pretty well stocked. However in 2009 the triploids planted were brook trout, not rainbows.

Gazetted name: Marquart Lake (data source: BC Ministry of Environment)

General location: East of Merritt

Surface area: 57 acres

Elevation: 3700 feet

Regulations: (readers consult current issue)

The dirt road leading to Marquart continues on past Marquart and leads to Lundbom Lake just a short distance farther. This makes it convenient to combine two lakes in one fishing trip.

See the following chart for details of the stocking history, noting that in 2009 the rainbow trout plant was diploids, not triploids as in the previous twelve years.

Marquart Lake Planting History				
Year	Rainbow	Rainbow	Brook Trout	Brook Trout
	Diploids	Triploids	Diploid	Triploid
1962	10,000			
1964	15,000			
1966	8,000			
1970			5,000	
1978			15,000	
1980	5,000		5,000	
1981	5,000		5,000	
1982	5,000		5,000	
1983	5,000		5,000	
1984	5,000			
1985	5,000		4,000	
1986	5,000		4,000	
1987	5,000		4,000	
1988	5,000		4,000	
1989	5,000		4,000	
1990	5,000		4,000	
1991	5,000		4,000	
1992	5,000		4,000	
1993	5,000		4,000	
1994	5,000		4,000	
1995	3,500			6,000
1996	4,500			4,000
1997		4,500		4,000
1998		4,500		4,000
1999		4,500		4,000
2000		4,500		4,000
2001		4,500		4,000
2002		4,499		4,500
2003		4,500		4,000
2004		4,500		4,000
2005		4,500		4,000
2006		4,500		4,000
2007		4,500		4,000
2008		4,500		4,000
2009	4,500			4,000

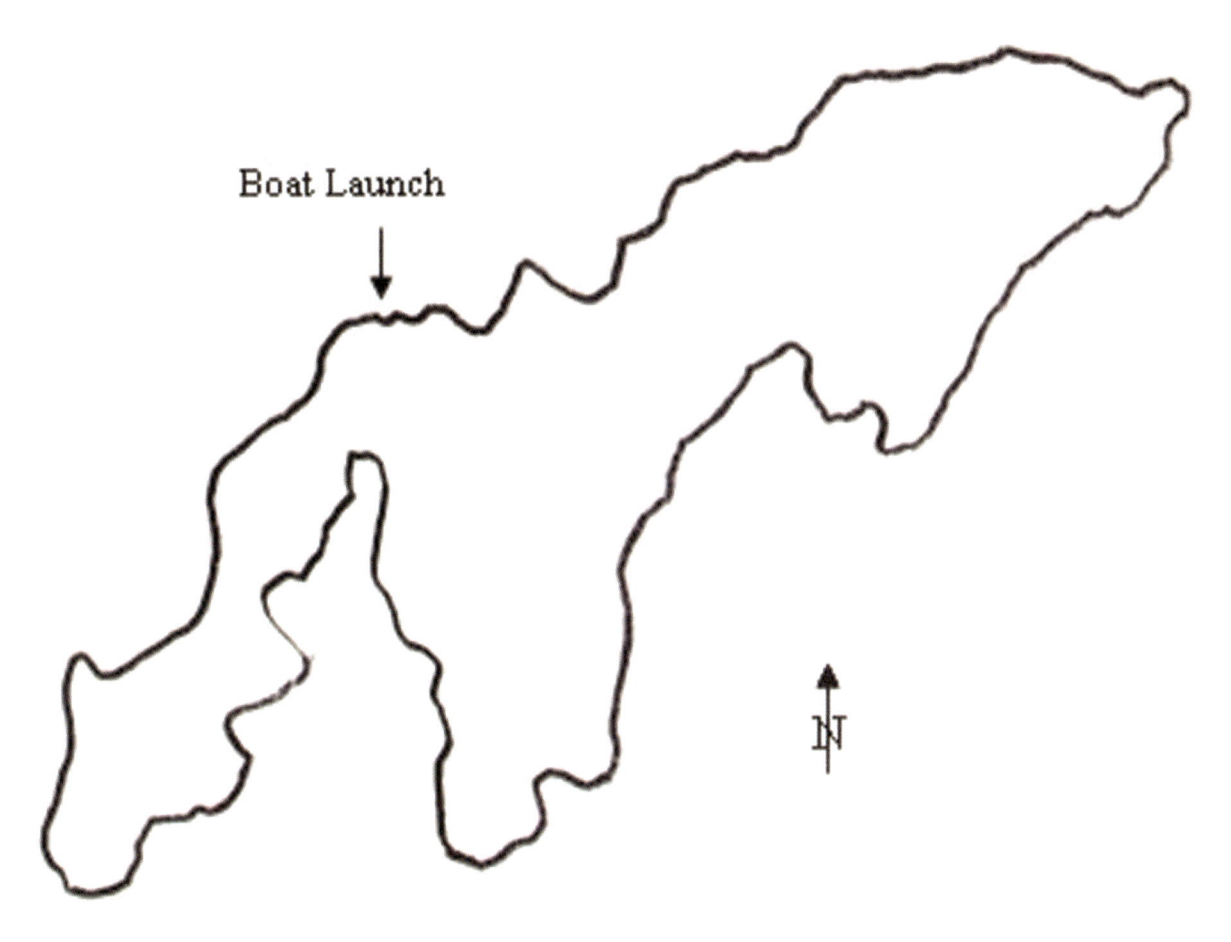

MINNIE LAKE

Minnie Lake is part of the Douglas Lake Ranch, as are several other lakes including Stoney, Salmon, Harry's Dam, Pikeshead, Damsel, and Crater. To find Minnie Lake, drive north on Highway 5A from the town of Merritt. About one mile north of the place called Quilchena, alongside Nicola Lake, there is a sign for Minnie Lake and Stoney Lake. Turn right onto the dirt road and follow it for about ten miles or so up to the locked security gates leading to Minnie and Stoney Lakes. You'll need the lock combination obtained when registering ahead of time for a trip to these lakes. You'll actually drive by Minnie on the way to Stoney Lake Lodge (there is no lodge on Minnie). It's only about two miles from Stoney back to Minnie for fishing.

There are a couple of places to launch boats on Minnie Lake, and the one that's farthest in along the western shore as best. Fishing seems best along the southwest shore of the lake in the eastern arm starting right at the point of land close to the launch area. I can still remember my first trip to Minnie some forty-five years ago. There was a profuse hatch of chironomids, and the big Kamloops trout were hitting hard.

Gazetted name: Minnie Lake (source BC maps)

General location: Northeast of Merritt

Surface area: 300 acres

Elevation: About 3600 feet

Maximum depth: Fairly shallow

Regulations: Private lake; follow Douglas Lake Ranch rules

To restore the fishing quality in Minnie and Stoney Lakes, the owners recently spent very substantial sums of money—about $750,000 to raise the levels of both lakes and then $500,000 to restock the two lakes each with 25,000 rainbows. A group I fished with in 2007 found that these improvements seem to be working successfully in both lakes.

This is a lake that every fly fisher should visit. There's lots of trout and they are big! A particularly effective fly is the chironomid in either the Ice Cream Cone or the Frosty patterns. Then too the Nyerges Nymph, Wooly Bugger, and Leech patterns have proven to be deadly. Much of the good fishing is found in relatively shallow areas. A fish finder/depth finder is quite useful to locate the drop offs in the lake.

The boats furnished and kept at Minnie Lake are rather heavy aluminum john boats. Oars and nets are provided and stored in boxes at the launch area.

PETERHOPE LAKE

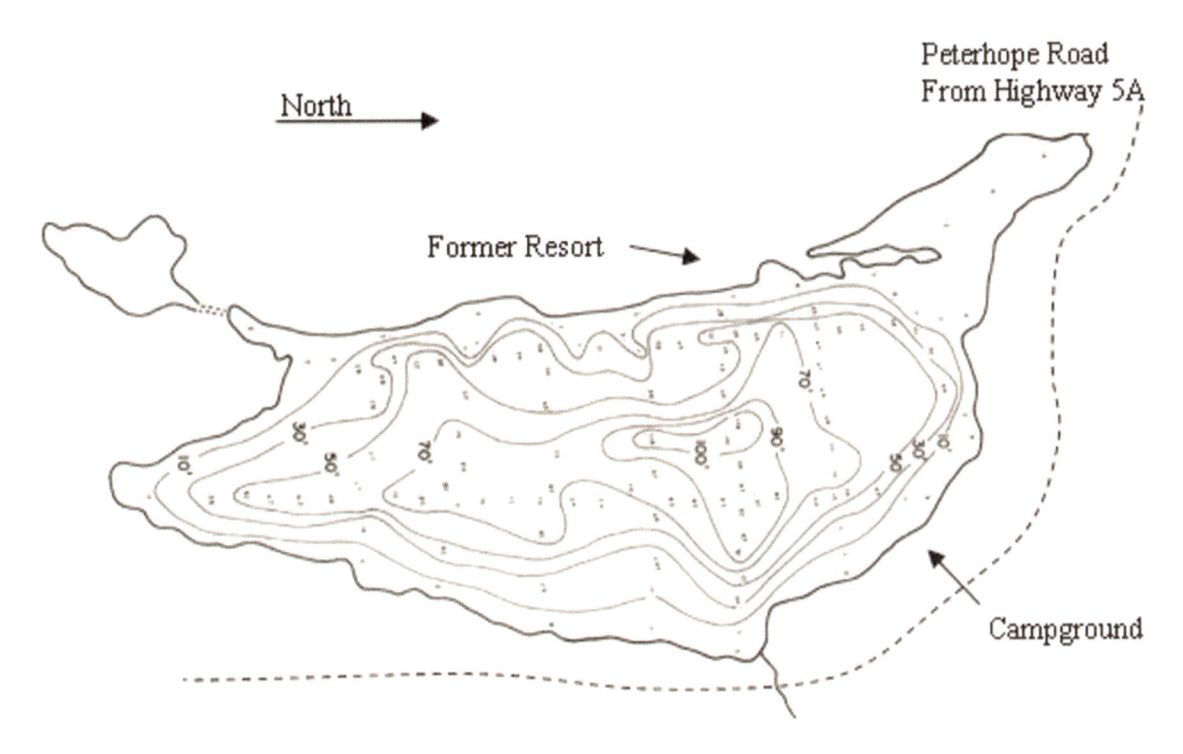

Peter Hope is one of the best known lakes in BC. It has been known to produce large fish for many years and is easily accessed. To find it, take Highway 5A north about eight miles past Nicola Lake, then turn off to the right at Peter Hope road and follow the dirt road about five miles to the lake. There used to be a resort on the west side of the lake, but that has closed and is being sold off as private property by Peter Hope Lake Resort Development Inc. There is a large camp ground on the northern shore of the lake with boat-launch facilities. It is heavily used. Note that the lake is quite open and subject to rough water from winds. To avoid crowds go on weekdays and avoid holidays.

Peter Hope is a beautiful lake with shoals, marl bottom, and good hatches, but it can be a tough lake to fish. Best flies include Leeches, Sedges, Half-Backs, chironomids, and Water Boatmen.

> Gazetted name: Peter Hope Lake (Source: BC Ministry of Environment)
> General location: North of Merritt
> Surface area: 287 acres
> Elevation: 3459 feet
> Maximum depth: 100 feet
> Regulations: (readers consult current issue)
>   1. Closed to fishing December 1through April 30
>   2. Limit: 2 fish daily
>   3. Bait ban, single barbless hook

A remarkable project called the Small Lakes Water Conservation Project was completed at Peter Hope Lake to protect the lake level from drawdown for agricultural purposes. It began in 1994 and was put together by the BC Environment Fisheries Branch with funding from the Habitat Conservation Trust Fund and the Interior Wetlands Program. Major players in this unique cooperative project included John Lauder, Jim LaBounty, the Gerard Guichon Ranch, Ducks

Unlimited, and Environment Canada. This model demonstration project included building new fences and cattle guards to exclude cattle from grazing in the riparian areas and the marsh north of the lake, and John Lauder provided a portion of his licensed summer range to be fenced off from cattle grazing. Then a new well, pump house, and watering facility were constructed to provide year-round watering for the livestock. The result of this work was a win-win for all parties. In 1997 the lake level reached spillway height for the first time in some thirty years. We owe our thanks to all who participated.

Fly fishers can expect to see the results of this work improving the fishing in Peter Hope Lake for many years to come.

For a summary of the fish stocking program, please see the following chart. Note that Peter Hope received a triploid plant in 2004, 2008, and 2009.

Peter Hope Lake Fish Stocking History						
Year	Diploids	Size	Year	Diploids	Triploids	Size
1932	10,000	Eggs	1976	25,000		
1936	10,095	Fry	1977	22,000		
1937	10,000	Fry	1978	25,000		
1938	10,000	Fry	1979	25,000		
1939	10,000	Fry	1980	25,000		
1940	20,000	Fry	1981	20,000		
1941	20,000	Fry	1986	30,000		
1952	30,000		1987	12,200		
1954	72,000	Fry	1988	35,000		
1956	72,000	Fry	1989	20,000		Yearling
1957	72,000	Fry	1990	20,000		Yearling
1959	8,000	Yearling	1992	20,000		Yearling
1960	14,500	Fry	1993	12,001		Yearling
1961	14,500	Fry	1994	12,000		Yearling
1962	22,000	Fry	1995	12,000		Yearling
1963	75,000	Fry/Yearling	1996	12,000		Yearling
1964	15,000	Fingerling	1997	12,000		Yearling
1965	25,000	Fry	1998	12,000		Yearling
1966	50,000	Fry	1999	12,000		Yearling
1968	20,000	Fingerling	2000	12,000		Yearling
1969	21,300	Fingerling	2001	12,000		Yearling
1970	40,000	Fry/Fingerling	2002	12,000		Yearling
1971	32,000	Fry/Fingerling	2003	12,000		Yearling
1972	25,000	Fingerling	2004	12,000	3,000	Yearling
1973	22,500	Yearling	2005	12,000		Yearling
1974	18,570	Fingerling	2006	12,000		Yearling
1975	30,000	Fingerling	2007	12,000		Yearling
			2008		12,000	Yearling
			2009		12,045	Yearling

PLATEAU LAKE

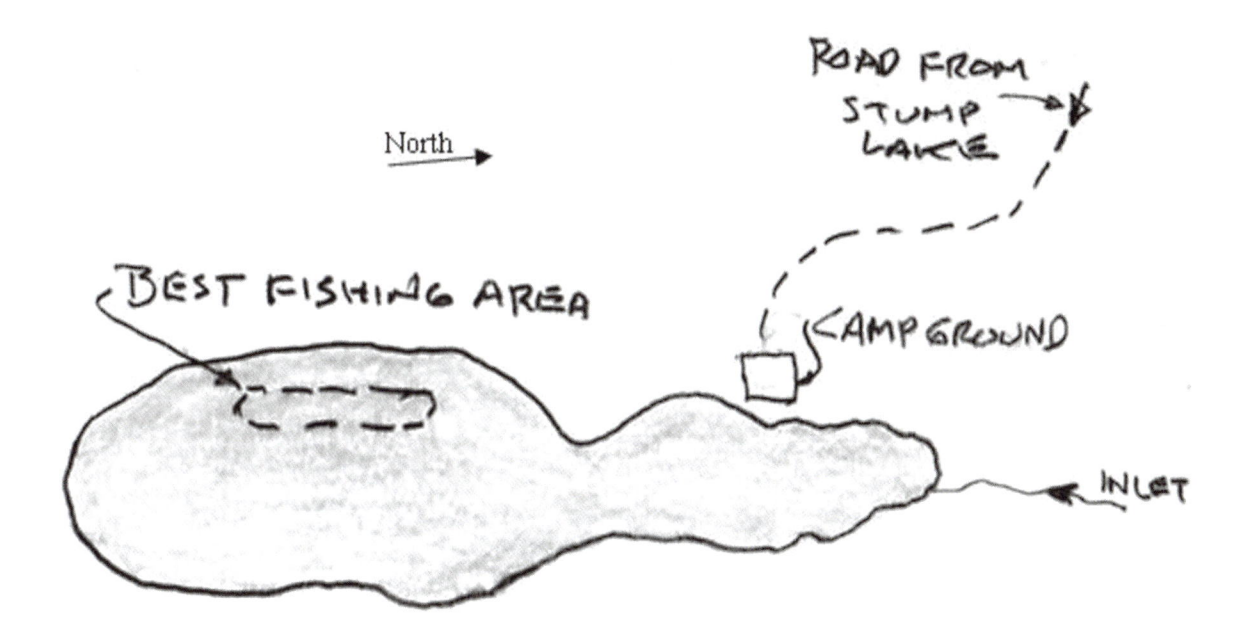

Plateau is a tough lake to get to because the road is rough with rocks and mud holes. A four-wheel-drive vehicle is recommended. The lake is located east of Stump Lake. There are two roads leading to Plateau, one from the north end of Stump Lake, the other off the east side of Peter Hope Lake. The latter is particularly rocky, steep, and rough.

Once at Plateau there is a nice forest service campground and a place to launch boats. There is no resort or cabins on the lake. Fishing is good in June and is noted for good fall fishing in September.

Gazetted name: Plateau Lake (data source: BC Ministry of Environment)
General location: east of Stump Lake
Surface area: 96 acres
Elevation: 3985 feet
Regulations: (readers consult current issue)
  1. Electric motors only

Plateau is stocked lightly with an annual plant of eight thousand yearlings to augment its natural recruitment. The Plateau ponds were also stocked with triploids in 2005. The Kamloops trout in this lake are beautiful fish—strong, hard, and full of fight. When the caddis hatch is on in June or July, it is indeed great fishing with a Tom Thumb, Elk Hair Caddis, Grizzly King, Black O'Lindsay, or Sedge Pupa.

See the chart following to review the stocking history of Plateau.

Plateau Lake Stocking History					
Year	Diploid	Triploid	Size		
1993	8,000		Yearlings		
1994	8,000		Yearlings		
1995	8,000		Yearlings		
1996	8,000		Yearlings		
1997	8,000		Yearlings		
1998	8,000		Yearlings		
1999	8,000		Yearlings		
2000	8,000		Yearlings		
2001	8,000		Yearlings		
2002	8,000		Yearlings		
2003	8,000		Yearlings		
2004	8,000		Yearlings		
2005	8,000		Yearlings		
2006	8,000		Yearlings		
2007	8,000		Yearlings		
2008	8,000		Yearlings		
2009	7,000		Yearlings		

Author (the one in the back of the boat) at Plateau Lake

ROCHE LAKE

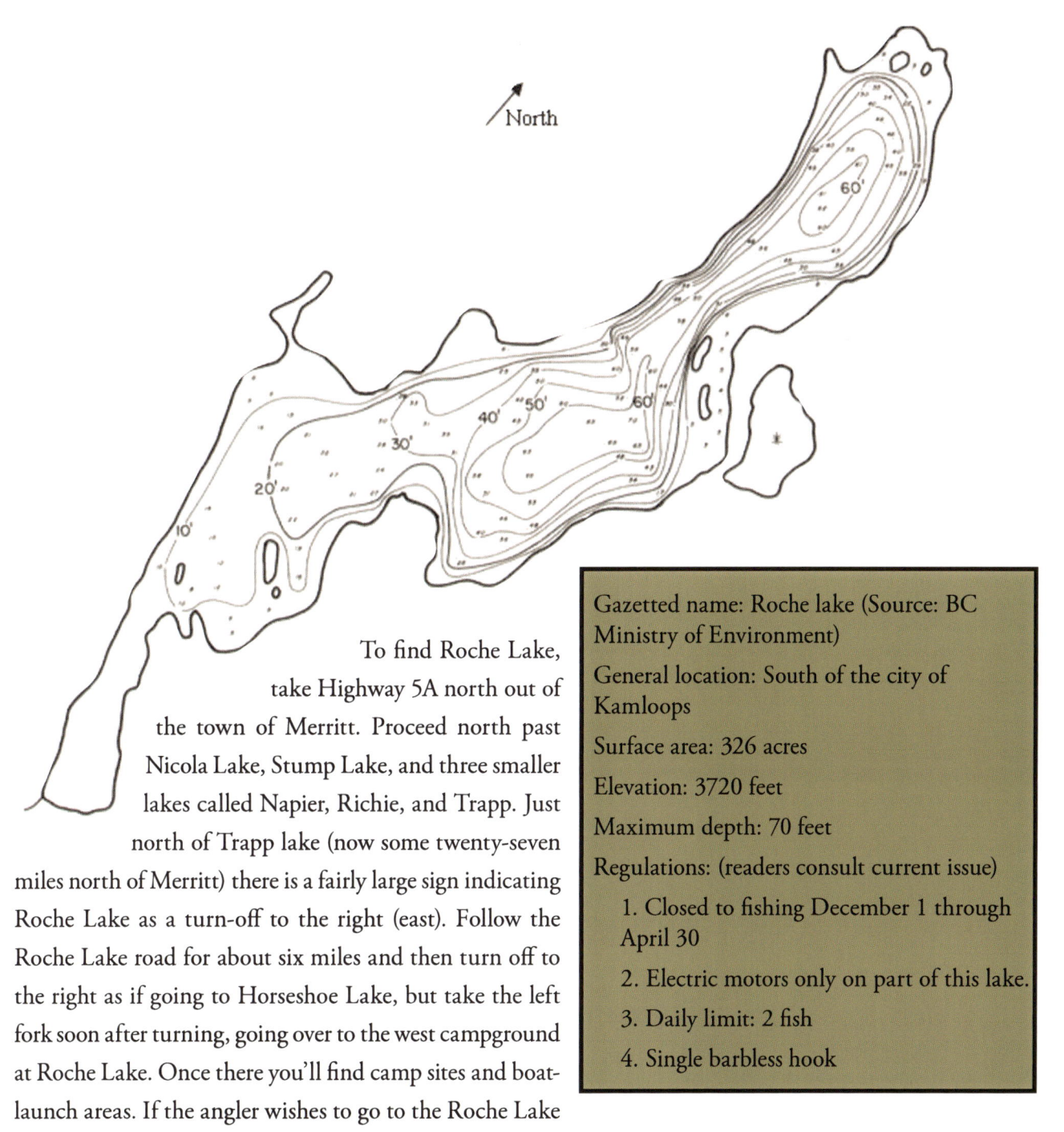

To find Roche Lake, take Highway 5A north out of the town of Merritt. Proceed north past Nicola Lake, Stump Lake, and three smaller lakes called Napier, Richie, and Trapp. Just north of Trapp lake (now some twenty-seven miles north of Merritt) there is a fairly large sign indicating Roche Lake as a turn-off to the right (east). Follow the Roche Lake road for about six miles and then turn off to the right as if going to Horseshoe Lake, but take the left fork soon after turning, going over to the west campground at Roche Lake. Once there you'll find camp sites and boat-launch areas. If the angler wishes to go to the Roche Lake Resort, do not turn off to Horseshoe lake but proceed straight ahead for another one and a half miles, then turn off to the right, following this road about three-quarters of a mile to the resort.

Gazetted name: Roche lake (Source: BC Ministry of Environment)

General location: South of the city of Kamloops

Surface area: 326 acres

Elevation: 3720 feet

Maximum depth: 70 feet

Regulations: (readers consult current issue)

1. Closed to fishing December 1 through April 30
2. Electric motors only on part of this lake.
3. Daily limit: 2 fish
4. Single barbless hook

Anglers would be well advised to try this lake. It is a nice sized lake for fly fishers. It is about three miles long by three-quarters mile wide. Roche is a well-used lake because it is located close to the city of Kamloops, so the angler can expect lots of company. Be aware too that the lake is within the Roche Lake Provincial Park, so camping fees apply. There are two camping areas, one on the west side of the lake and the other at the north end. The Roche Lake Resort is located on the east side of the lake and provides cabins and facilities.

Roche has interesting contours; the lake is deep enough to prevent winter kills. There are also four islands in the lake that serve to make it interesting. Roche is known for good chironomid fishing and excellent caddis fly hatches, and in the fall the Boatman hatch can be exciting.

The heavy triploid plant in this lake over the last four years bodes well for the opportunity for angler's to catch large fish.

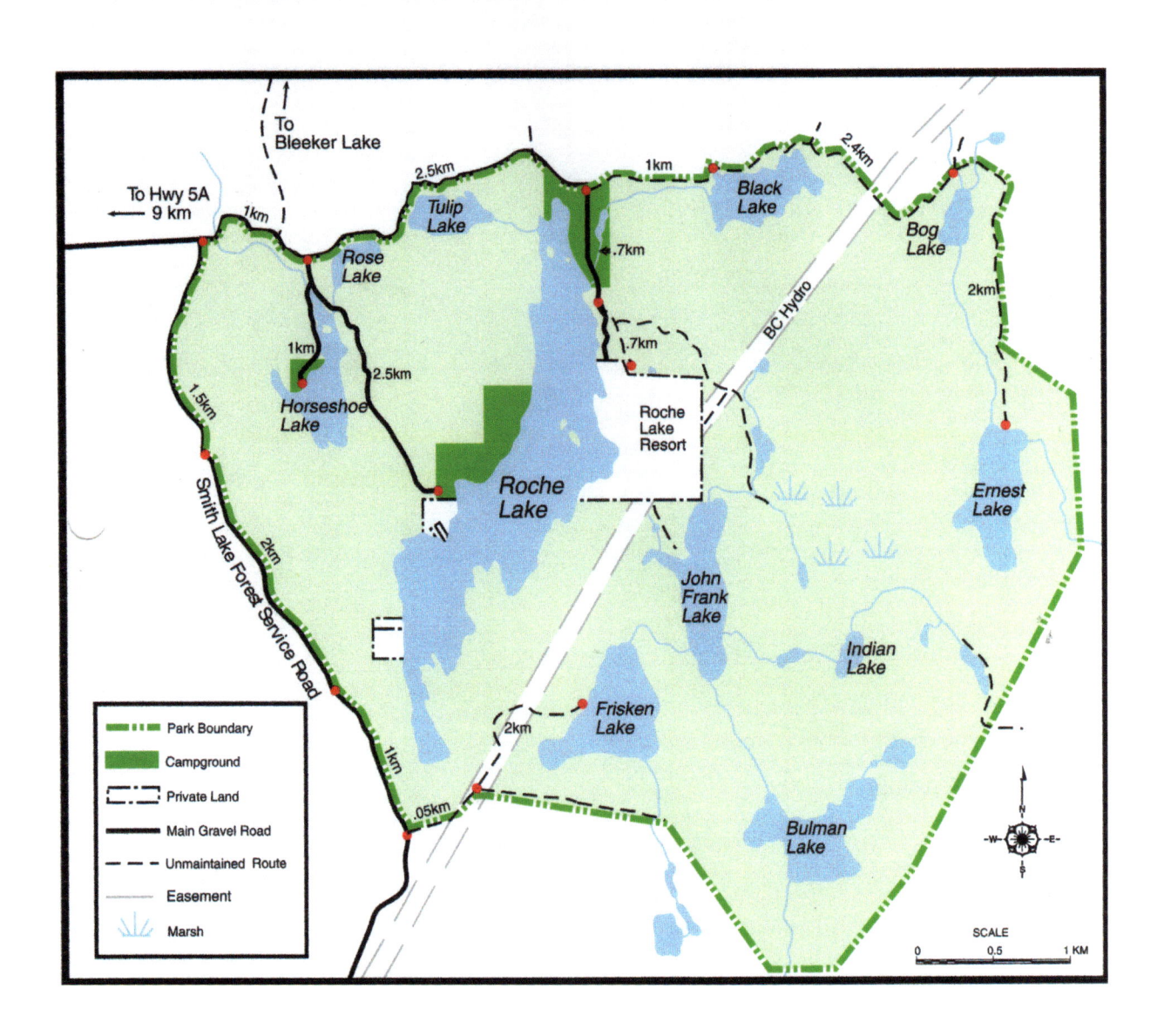

For the fish stocking history of this lake, see the chart below:

Roche lake Stocking History						
Year	Diploids	Stage	Year	Diploids	Triploids	Stage
1952	12,000	Fry	1985	45,000		
1958	5,000	Fingerling	1986	45,000		
1966	80,000	Fry	1987	51,000		
1968	155,000	Fry & Fingrl	1988	45,000		
1969	30,000	Fingerling	1989	45,000		Yearling
1970	45,000	Fingerling	1990	45,000		Yearling
1971	35,000	Fingerling	1991	45,000		Yearling
1972	45,000	Fingerling	1992	50,000		Yearling
1973	45,500	Fingerling	1993	45,000		Yearling
1974	45,000	Fingerling	1994	46,725		Yearling
1975	45,000	Fingerling	1995	45,000		Yearling
1976	45,000		1996	35,000		Yearling
1977	45,000		1997	35,000		Yearling
1978	85,800		1998	35,000		Yearling
1979	65,000		1999	35,000		Yearling
1980	65,000		2000	35,000		Yearling
1981	65,000		2001	25,000		Yearling
1982	60,000		2002	25,000		Yearling
1983	60,000		2003	25,000		Yearling
1984	60,000		2004	22,500	12,500	Yearling
			2005	15,000	7,500	Yearling
			2006	15,000	17,500	Yearling
			2007	15,000	7,500	Yearling
			2008	14,993	7,496	Yearling
			2009	15,000	7,500	Yearling

STONEY LAKE

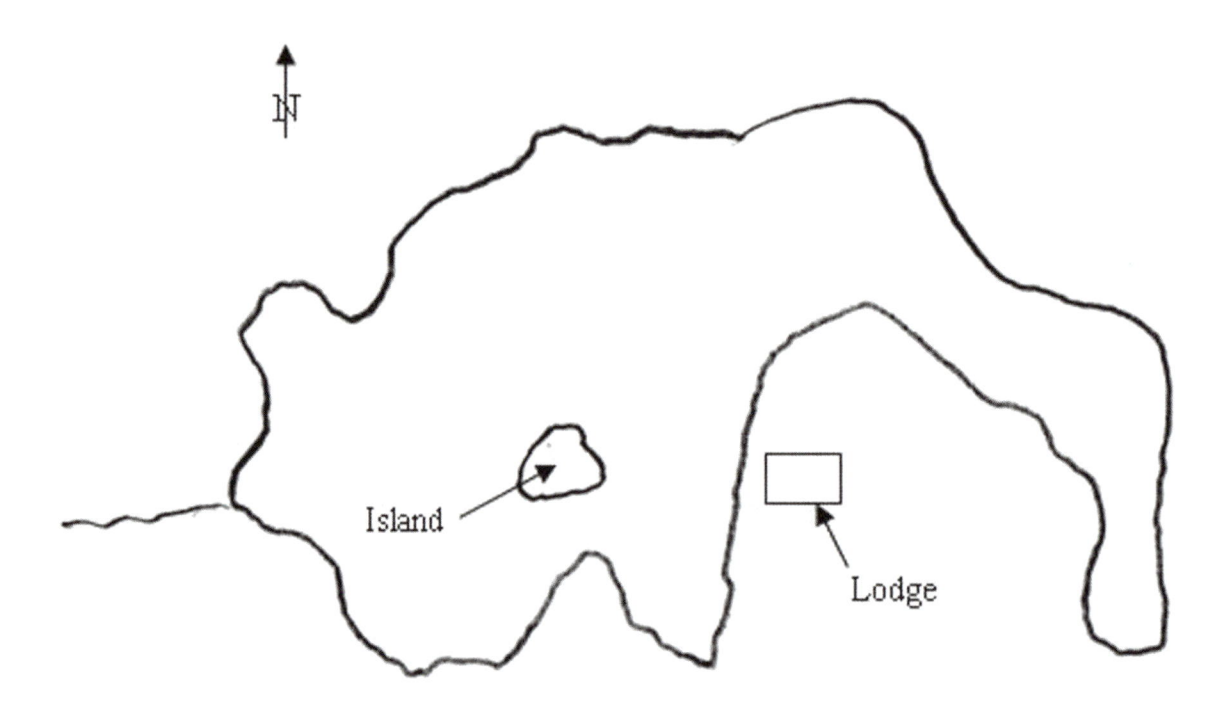

Stoney Lake Lodge is part of the Douglas Lake Ranch. To find Stoney Lake, take Highway 5A north out of the town of Merritt. About one mile past the place called Quilchena, alongside Lake Nicola, there is a right-hand turn sign that points to a dirt road. From there it's about ten miles up to the locked security gates leading to Stoney and Minnie Lakes. You'll need the combination to the lock given to you when registering for a stay at the lodge. Then it's only a short drive past Minnie and on to Stoney. The lodge is nicely situated and provides the angler with rooms, meals, and boats.

> Gazetted name: Stoney Lake (source BC maps)
> General location: Northeast of Merritt
> Surface Area: About 150 acres
> Elevation: About 3600 feet
> Regulations: Private lake; follow Douglas Lake Ranch rules

Home of two famous lakes, Minnie and Stoney, the lodge at Stoney Lake offers much to the fly fisher. This facility at Stoney Lake is a lovely modern lodge about ten yrs old. They furnish rooms, meals, boats, anchors, and nets, and the lodge provides access to several lakes to fish, including Stoney, Minnie, Harry's Dam, Pikeshead, Salmon, Sabin, Damsel, Crater, and Wasley. These lakes are private and are controlled by the Douglas Lake Ranch. Reservations are required, and access is through a locked gate. The ranch has spent considerable funds in 2005, 2006 and 2007 to raise the water levels on Minnie and Stoney Lakes and to plant fish (25,000 were planted in 2006). It is expected that fishing beginning in 2007 will once again be very good and that the fish will be large.

During 2007, the fish my party took in the spring were running about eighteen inches long. There is a boat launch area close to the lodge for those wishing to use their own boats. Take your camera along to take photos of the big fish and also to take some snapshots of the Canada geese nesting on the small island.

Good areas to fish are off the island, along the north shore, and down into the east leg of the lake. Here again a fish finder/depth finder is a very useful tool when exploring this lake. Note too that the east leg can sometimes offer the angler protection from a stiff wind. Chironomids and leeches work well anywhere in the lake. Two patterns that have proven successful in the main body of the lake are the Byrd's Black Magic and the Maroon Marabou Leech (see the chapter "Must-have Flies"). The angler can expect big fish—and lots of them.

Fish planting records are not available because it is a private lake. Stoney and Minnie Lakes, like the other private lakes on the Douglas Lake Ranch, are not listed in the sport fishing regulations. However the owners cater to fly fishers and practice catch and release.

Stump Lake

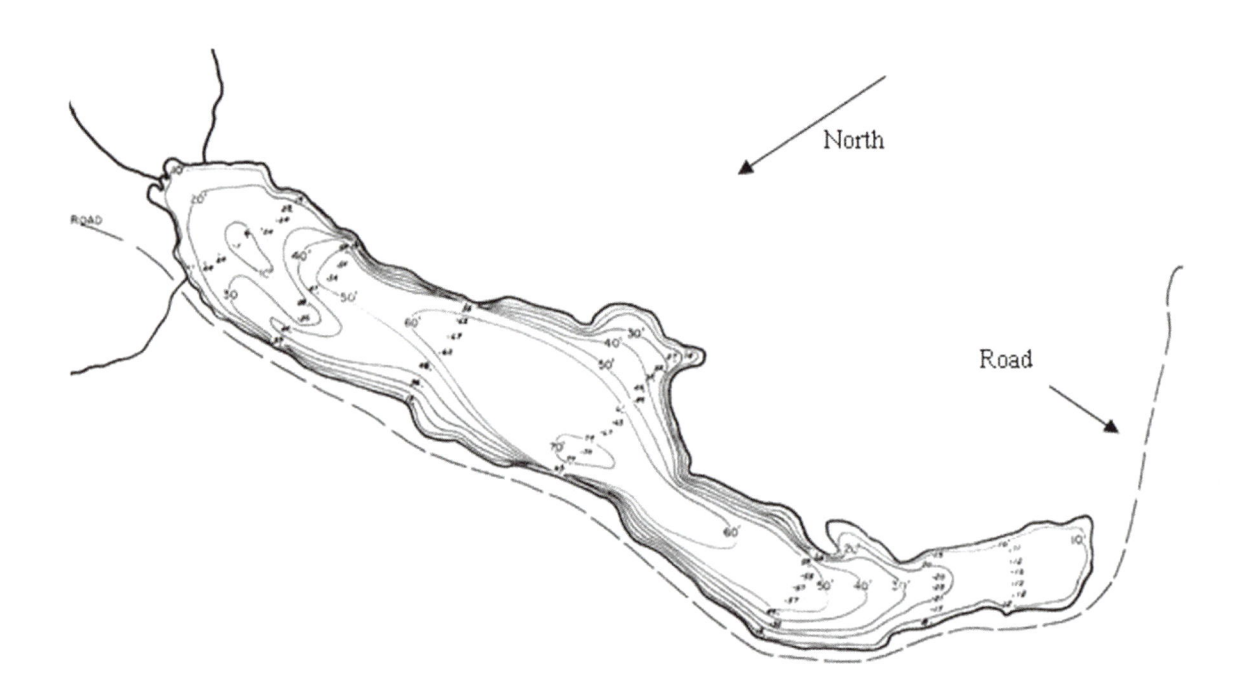

Stump Lake has long been one of the fabled lakes of British Columbia. To reach the lake, take Highway 5A north from the town of Merritt about thirty miles. The road passes right alongside the lake. There is one crude boat launching area about halfway up the length of the lake. Stump is a large and very open lake, with no shelter for the wind. Thus it is wise to use a good sized boat and a motor. Keep an eye out for inclement weather.

The first I heard about Stump Lake was probably thirty years ago when Ted Trueblood wrote an article in one of the fly fishing magazines describing the huge trout he had taken there. The lake is still good, although like many lakes it has its on and off days. Stump has been planted with huge numbers of trout over the years; for example, 326,000 rainbow trout were planted in 1963. During the '70s and '80s the lake was planted with Kokanee and brook trout in addition to rainbow trout. However, beginning in the '90s Stump Lake was planted with only rainbows and Kokanee trout. Triploid rainbow trout were introduced in 1997 and have been planted every year since. Even though this lake is quite large at 1928 acres, the fish density is reasonably high. In 2008 160,000 rainbows were planted, amounting to 83 fish per acre,

Gazetted name: Stump Lake (Source: BC Ministry of Environment)
General location: 30 miles north of Merritt
Surface Area: 1928 acres
Elevation: 2460 feet
Maximum depth: 70 feet
Regulations: (readers consult current issue)
  1. Speed restriction: 70 km/hr (43 mph)

or 114 fish per acre if Kokanee trout were included. Note too that 78 percent of the rainbow trout planted in 2008 were triploids and 66 percent of the Kokanee were triploids.

Stump is renowned for its fabulous bug hatches. There are shallow areas on both ends of the lake where good fly fishing may be had using damsels, sedges, or leeches.

See the following chart for the fish planting history of this lake.

Stump Lake Fish Planting History									
Year				Year	Rainbow Diploid	Triploid	Kokanee Diploid	Triploid	Brook
	Rainbow	Kokanee	Brook						
1911	10,000 cuts			1984	150,000		265,760		100,000
1955	10,000			1985	60,000		50,000		
1956	75,000			1986	293,400		77,000		
1959	200,500			1987	247,000		200,000		50,000
1960	160,000			1988	140,000		200,000		50,000
1961	85,000			1989	100,000		250,000		99,000
1962	100,000			1990	70,000		260,000		50,000
1963	326,000			1991	155,747				
1964	11,100			1992	104,133		200,000		
1966	98,000			1993	128,849		200,000		
1967	10,000			1994	191,509		1,500		
1968	50,000			1996	137,756				
1969	100,000			1997	81,049	122,485	229,500		
1970	200,000			1998	40,000	54,928	150,000		
1971	166,000			1999	91,922	47,824	100,000		
1972	175,000			2000	60,000	35,000	65,000		
1973	134,000			2001	98,131	59,993			
1974	50,000			2002	60,000	73,785	65,000		
1975	50,000			2003	72,012	73,032	85,000		
1976	75,000	27,000		2004	60,000	35,560	85,000	30,255	
1977	231,000	50,000		2005	60,200	46,100	60,000	60,014	
1978	241,000	95,150		2006	70,489	40,000	61,000	61,000	
1979	195,000	100,000		2007	60,000	40,000	31,860	20,740	
1980	75,000		75,000	2008	35,000	125,000	20,000	40,002	
1981	127,750		50,000	2009	192,032	78,834	40,000	40,000	
1982	185,100	150,500							
1983	74,000	89,250	53,000						

Sullivan Lake (also known as Knouff Lake)

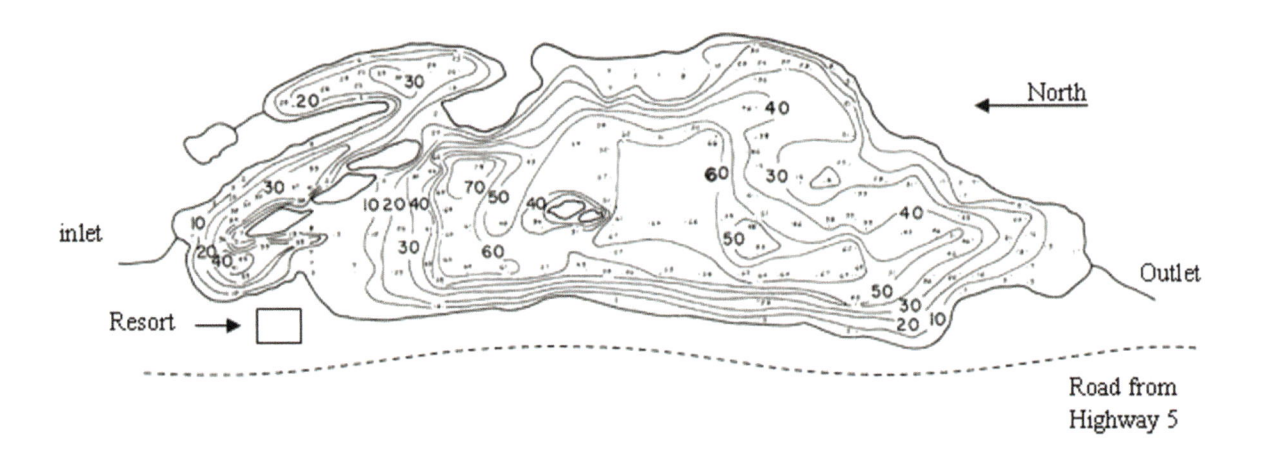

Sullivan Lake is an interesting lake to fish. This lake is found by taking Highway 5 for fifteen miles north out of Kamloops and then turning right onto the Heffley Creek Road. After traveling about three miles, turn to the left on a forestry road and take it about nine miles to the lake. This road goes up along the west side of Sullivan and leads both to the Knouff Lake Resort and to a campground and recreation site located about half\ way up the lake. The recreation site is west of the road while the lake is east of the road. This recreation site will accommodate campers, trailers, and RVs. The boat launch area is across the road.

What makes this lake interesting to fly fishers is the fabulous sedge fly hatches in the spring, and the several islands around which to fish. The deepest spot in the lake is some sixty-eight feet north of the two islands. Some of the more successful fly patterns include chironomids, mayflies, sedges, shrimp, leeches, and boatman.

Gazetted name: Sullivan Lake (Knouff) (Source: BC Ministry of Environment)

General location: Northeast of Kamloops

Surface area: 252 acres

Elevation: 3768 feet

Maximum depth: 70 feet

Regulations: (readers consult current issue)
  1. Daily limit: 2 rainbow trout
  2. Single hook

The planting history of this lake is interesting because it has been planted most every year since 1930. In the early years (1933, 1935, 1936) it received heavy plants of 150,000 rainbows, and in 1951, 1952, and 1953 it received 100,000 rainbows each year. Then beginning in 1998 the lake received 1,000 triploids along with 4,000 diploids each year for five years in a row. No planting was done for the years 2004–2009 because natural production has been more than sufficient to sustain the lake. See the following recap.

\multicolumn{3}{l	}{Sullivan (Knouff) Lake Planting History}			
Year	Diploid	Triploid	Year	Diploid	Year
2009	0	0			
2008	0	0			
2007	0	0	1982	15,000	1955	5,000
2006	0	0	1981	10,000	1954	6,000
2005	0	0	1980	15,000	1953	100,000
2004	0	0	1979	15,000	1952	100,000
2003	4,000	0	1978	15,000	1951	100,000
2002	4,000	1,000	1977	20,000	1950	75,000
2001	4,000	1,000	1976	20,000	1949	75,000
2000	4,000	1,000	1975	20,000	1947	75,000
1999	4,000	1,000	1974	15,100	1946	75,000
1998	4,000	1,000	1973	27,000	1945	75,000
1997	7,000		1972	40,000	1944	75,000
1996	8,000		1971	40,000	1943	50,000
1995	8,000		1970	40,000	1942	50,000
1994	10,000		1969	40,000	1941	50,000
1993	10,000		1968	20,000	1940	50,000
1992	16,000		1966	22,000	1939	60,000
1990	10,000		1965	10,000	1938	50,000
1989	6,000		1963	18,000	1937	5,000
1988	6,000		1962	9,000	1936	150,000
1987	6,000		1961	11,000	1935	150,000
1986	6,000		1960	20,000	1934	35,117
1985	6,000		1959	12,000	1933	150,000
1984	6,000		1957	72,000	1932	133,975
1983	6,000		1956	85,000	1930	30,000

Tunkwa Lake

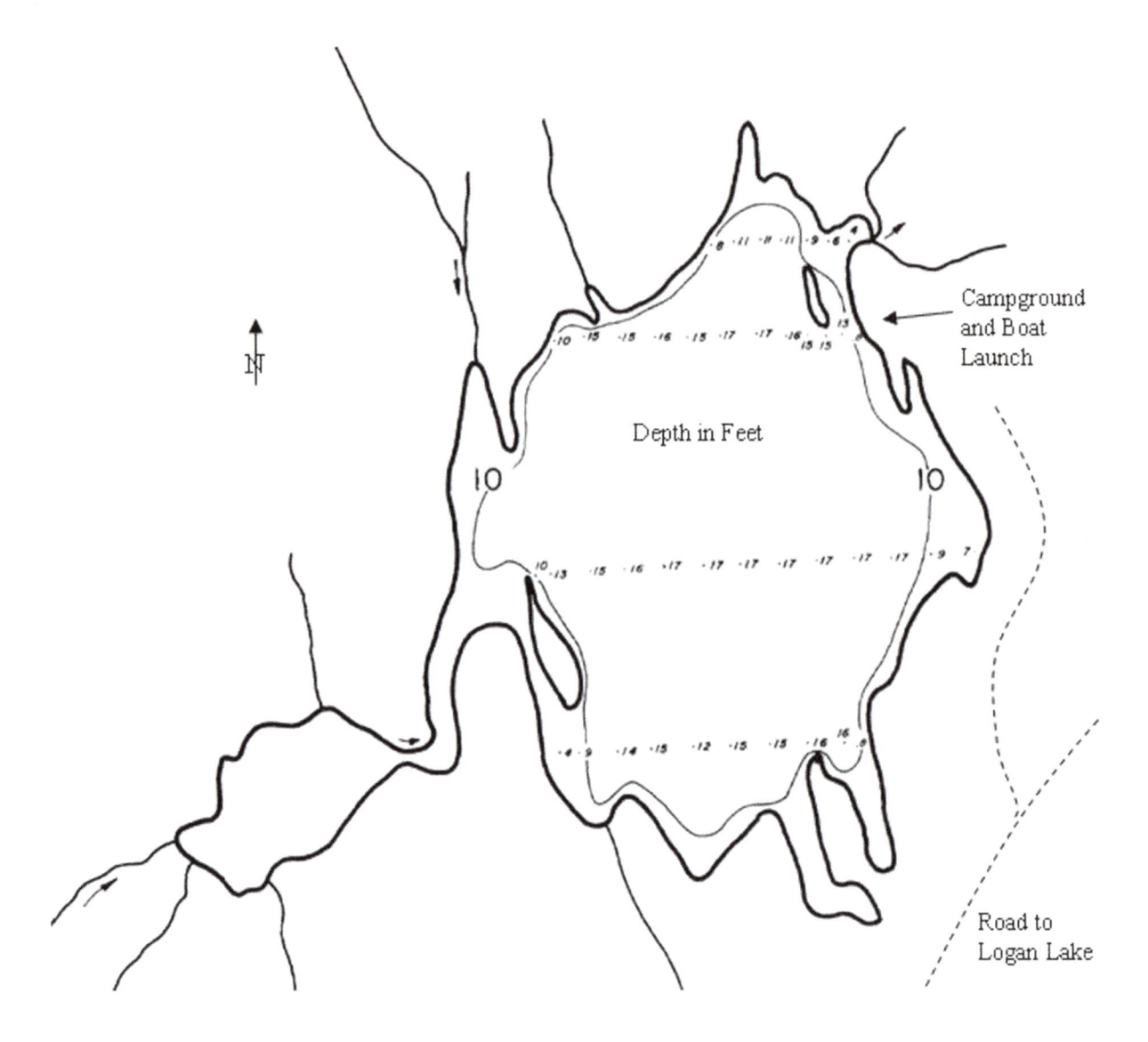

Tunkwa is a rather large but not very deep lake located within Tunkwa Provincial Park. It is situated about ten miles north of the town of Logan Lake. As such it is provided with a large campground on the northeast side of the lake that can accommodate tents, truck campers, trailers, and RVs. Services are offered for fifteen dollars per night per party from May 1 to October 8.

Tunkwa has been rather heavily stocked for many years, receiving about forty to fifty thousand yearling rainbows each year for the past fifteen years. As part of the 2006–2009 plants the lake received fifteen to twenty-five thousand triploids.

Gazetted name: Tunkwa Lake (source: BC Ministry of Environment)

General location: North of Logan Lake

Surface area: 730 acres

Elevation: 3751 feet

Maximum depth: 17 feet

Regulations: (readers consult latest issue)
  1. Closed to fishing December 1 through April 30
  2. Engine power restricted to 10 HP
  3. Provincial fishing license required

This lake is well utilized, so the angler can expect company. Nonetheless it is well-known for its heavy chironomid hatches and for trout that often jump high in the air, startling the fly fishers. Needless to say the chironomid patterns work well, as do shrimp and leeches.

See the following chart for the fish planting history.

Tunkwa Lake Stocking History					
Year	Diploids	Triploids	Total	Year	Diploids
2009	15,000	25,049AF	40,049		
2008	19,989	20,000	39,989		
2007	25,164	15,000	40,164	1974	55,000
2006	25,074	15,000	40,074	1973	40,500
2005	40,000			1972	45,000
2004	50,050			1971	45,000
2003	49,949			1970	45,000
2002	50,237			1969	45,000
2001	50,065			1968	24,000
2000	52,736			1967	24,000
1999	49,350			1966	30,000
1998	49,864			1964	40,000
1997	49,438			1963	32,000
1996	56,062			1962	32,000
1995	56,240			1961	13,000
1994	55,930			1960	23,000
1993	70,400			1959	11,500
1992	70,159			1958	9,200
1991	70,000			1956	46,500
1990	65,618			1955	46,500
1989	69,832			1954	47,500
1988	90,722			1953	25,000
1987	115,000			1952	100,000
1986	80,000			1951	100,000
1985	50,000			1950	25,000
1984	70,000			1949	25,000
1983	70,000			1948	40,000
1982	95,000			1947	25,000
1981	70,000			1946	30,000
1980	70,000			1945	10,000
1979	70,000			1944	10,000
1978	70,000			1943	20,000
1977	60,000			1942	20,000
1976	55,000			1941	20,000
1975	55,000			1940	20,000
				1939	15,000

Chapter 4

Must-Have Flies

My Three Favorite Flies

The Green Bodied Tom Thumb

The Nyerges Nymph

76

The Black O'Lindsay

These three flies are the best of the best. When the caddis (sedge) hatch is on, it's very hard to beat the Green Bodied Tom Thumb dry fly.

For all-around fly fishing in any of the lakes in British Columbia, the Nyerges Nymph is my favorite. It doesn't seem to matter where I go; that fly really is effective. It is fished on a sink tip fly line by anchoring on the edge of a drop-off, then casting into shallow water and stripping out toward the deep. It works equally well on a sinking line or with a floating line. I'd estimate that something like 90 percent of the fish I take are caught on the Nyerges Nymph. The reason is that it imitates a shrimp and, to some extent, a caddis pupa, which are common food sources for the Kamloops trout. Reviewing records kept over the years at our annual Memorial Day fish-out at Glimpse Lake shows that 44 percent of the time the Nyerges Nymph caught the largest fish.

A really good evening fly is the Black O' Lindsay. It proves to be deadly when fished on a floating line or on a sink tip over the shoals from dusk till dark. This is the fly I caught my first big Kamloops trout on at Glimpse Lake, and that experience transformed me into a fly fisher forever.

MUST-HAVE FLY PATTERNS

Shown here are fifty-seven of the most successful fly patterns to use for catching Kamloops trout. There are hundreds of patterns from which to choose, but these are proven flies used by many expert fly fishers. Most anglers find they have many patterns in their tackle box that are seldom or rarely used, perhaps with a certain hatch. On the other hand, one needs to have the pattern to match the hatch. These flies have turned out to be steady producers over years of experience. If you have these in your tackle box, you'll almost always have what's needed. Below the photograph you'll see tying instructions for those who can tie their own.

DRY FLIES

ELK HAIR CADDIS FLY

Hook = Tiemco 100, size 12–14

Thread = tan monochord

Tail = none

Body = Tan dubbing

Hackle = Brown, palmered

Wing = Elk hair

TOM THUMB, STANDARD

Hook = Tiemco 5212, size 12

Thread = Black

Tail = Deer hair

Overwing = Deer hair tied in at back

Body = pull deer hair forward to form overwing and body

Overwing = pull forward, keeping the material on top of the hook; tie off right behind hook eye.

Tom Thumb Green Body

Hook = Tiemco 5212 size 12

Thread = Black nylon

Tail = Deer hair

Shell back = Deer hair pulled over body then tied down in front, long enough to make wing in front.

Body = Sparkly green yarn or dubbing

ADAMS

Hook = Tiemco 5212 size 14–16

Tying thread = Black nylon

Tail = Brown hackle fibers

Body = Fine gray yarn

Wings = Two grizzly tips upright and divided

Hackle = Brown hackle tied dry and full

ROYAL WULFF

Hook = Temco 5212 size 12–16

Tying thread = Black nylon

Tail = Deer hair

Butt = Peacock herl

Body = Red floss

Shoulder = Peacock herl

Wing = White calves, tail upright and divided

Hackle = Brown hackle tied dry and full

MOSQUITO

Hook = Tiemco 5212 size 14–16

Tying thread = Black nylon

Tail = Grizzly hackle fibers

Body = Grizzly quill

Wings = Two grizzly hackle tips upright and divided

Hackle = Grizzly tied dry and full

RED HUMPY

Hook = Tiemco 100 or Mustad 94840 size 12–14

Tying Thread = Black nylon

Tail = Brown hackle fibers

Wing case = Deer hair pulled over top after body is made; tie down in front; coat with head cement

Body = Red yarn

Hackle = Brown tied dry, dull side forward

Head = Small tapered

YELLOW HUMPY

Hook = Tiemco 100 or Mustad 94840 size 12–14

Tying thread = Black nylon

Tail = Brown hackle fibers

Wing case = Deer hair pulled over top after body is made;, tie down in front, coat with head cement

Hackle = Brown tied dry, dull side forward

Head = Small tapered

BLACK ANT

Hook = Tiemco 100 or Mustad 94840 size 12–14

Tying thread = Black

Tail = None

Body = Black yarn or black foam

Hackle = Brown tied at front.

Head = Tie in a piece of black foam on top of hook; then tie off with thread to make very small head

BROWN SEDGE

Hook = Tiemco 5212 size 10–12

Thread = Black or brown nylon

Tail = Brown hackle fibers

Body = Brown yarn or dubbing

Wing = Pheasant tail feather fibers

Hackle = Brown tied dry with dull side forward

Eye = Tapered black thread

WET FLIES

BLACK O'LINDSAY

Hook = Tiemco 200R size 8–10

Tying thread = Black or light green

Tail = Brown and blue hackle fibers mixed

Rib = Gold tinsel

Body = Yellow yarn

Hackle = Brown tied down as a beard

Under wing = Peacock sword feather fibers

Wing = Two mallard feathers laid exactly one on top of the other, length of body and tail

Head = Tapered black or light green thread

GRIZZLY KING

Hook = Tiemco 200R size 8–10

Tying thread = Light green nylon

Tail = Red hackle fibers

Rib = Gold tinsel

Body = Light green yarn

Hackle = Grizzly tied down

Wing = Two mallard breast feathers laid one on top of other

Head = Tapered green thread

Self Carey

Hook = Tiemco 200R size 8–10

Tying Thread = Black nylon

Tail = Pheasant rump feather fibers

Body = Pheasant rump feather twisted into noodle and wound on

Hackle = Pheasant rump feather with blue or green cast to color, 3–4 turns

Head = Tapered black thread

BLACK CAREY

Hook = Tiemco 200R size 8–10

Tying thread = Black

Tail = Pheasant rump feather with blue gray cast to color

Body = Black yarn, tapered

Hackle = Pheasant rump feather with blue gray cast to color, 3–4 turns

Head = Tapered black thread

Pink Carey

Hook = Tiemco 200R size 8–10

Thread = Black nylon

Tail = Pheasant rump feather fibers

Body = Light pink yarn

Hackle = Pheasant rump feather 3–4 turns only

Head = Black nylon tapered

PEACOCK CAREY

Hook = Tiemco 200R size 8–10

Thread = Black nylon

Tail = Pheasant rump feather fibers blue/green cast

Body = Peacock herl or sword feather

Hackle = Pheasant rump feather blue cast, 3–4 turns only.

Head = Black nylon tying thread tapered.

Green Carey

Hook = Tiemco 200R size 8–10

Tying thread = Olive green nylon

Tail = Pheasant rump feather blue green cast

Body = Insect green yarn

Hackle = Pheasant rump feather blue green cast, 3–4 turns

Head = Olive green thread, tapered

RED CAREY

Hook = Tiemco 200R size 8–10

Thread = Red nylon

Tail = Pheasant rump feather fibers

Body = Bright red yarn

Hackle = Pheasant rump feather 3–4 turns

Head = Red nylon tying thread, tapered

Watson's Anomaly

Created by Wilbur Watson, said to imitate "exactly nothing," but it works!

Hook = Tiemco 200R size 8–10

Thread = Black or red nylon

Tail = Burgundy marabou, also palmered up over chenille body

Body = Burgundy chenille

Wing = Burgundy marabou with crystal flash strands mixed in

Head = Tying thread, tapered

BUTT UGLY

Hook = Tiemco 200R size 10

Tying thread = Gray nylon

Tail = Pheasant rump feather blue gray cast

Body = Pheasant rump feather with blue gray cast, twisted into noodle and wound forward; leave some fibers sticking out of body

Hackle = Pheasant rump feather with blue-gray cast tied down as beard to point of hook

Head = Tying thread, tapered

Imitates a shrimp

SHRIMP

Hook = Tiemco 3761 or Mustad 94840

size 10–12

Tying thread = Black nylon

Tail = Brown hackle fibers

Shell back = Scud back material

Palmering = Brown hackle tied wet

Body = Green yarn, then palmer hackle, pull

scud back over top, tie off at front

Head = Tying thread, tapered

BLACK WOOLY BUGGER

Hook = Tiemco 300R or Mustad 3665A size 8–10

Thread = Black nylon

Tail = Clump of black marabou

Hackle = Black with fairly short fibers palmered forward

Body = Black chenille medium

Head = Black tying thread

Black Marabou Leech

Hook = Tiemco 300R or Mustad 3665A size 8–10

Thread = Black nylon

Tail = None

Body = Black chenille medium

Wing = Black marabou quite long, tie in at two places

on top of body, matuka style

Head = Black tying thread, fairly large tapered head

DR. SPRATLEY

Originated in 1949 by Dick Prankard; named after a dentist, Dr. Don Spratley. One of BC's most popular patterns.

Hook = Tiemco 200R size 8–10 or Mustad 9671

Tying thread = Black nylon

Tail = Grizzly hackle fibers

Rib = Silver tinsel narrow

Body = Black yarn

Hackle = Grizzly tied down as beard

Wing = Ring-necked pheasant tail fibers

Shoulder = Peacock herl

Head = Black tying thread

SPLIT WING SPRATLEY

Tying instructions same as above, but wing is

split to form a V. This variation seems to attract more fish.

GREEN SPRATLEY

Hook = Tiemco 200R or Mustad 9671 size 8–10

Tying thread = Light olive green

Tail = Grizzly

Rib = Silver tinsel

Body = Bright green yarn

Wing = Ring-necked pheasant tail feather fibers

Hackle = Grizzly tied down as beard

Shoulder = Peacock herl

Head = Tying thread

Thuya Spratley

Used at Thuya Lake.

Hook = Tiemco 200R or Mustad 9671 size 8–10

Tying thread = Red nylon

Tail = Ring-necked pheasant tail fibers, or grizzly

Rib = Silver tinsel

Body = Red yarn

Wing = Ring-necked pheasant tail fibers

Hackle = Grizzly tied down as beard

Shoulder = Peacock herl

Head = Red tying thread

SPLIT WING THUYA

Tying instructions same as for Thuya Spratley except wing is split to form a V.

CITATION SPRATLEY

Hook = Tiemco 200R or Mustad 9671 size 8–10

Tying thread = Black nylon

Rib = Silver or gold tinsel

Body = Light green "Citation" yarn

Wing = Ring-necked pheasant tail fibers

Hackle = Grizzly tied down as beard

Shoulder = None

Head = Black tying thread

DAMSEL

Hook = Tiemco 5212, 200R, Daiichi 1280 Size 8–10

Tying thread = Light olive green

Tail = Olive marabou

Rib = Fine gold tinsel

Body = Thin green yarn or dubbing

Wing case = Scud back

Wings = Split parallel to body, turkey

Thorax = Build up with dubbing or yarn

Eyes = Black mono

Wing case = Tie in first before wings, then

pull forward and tie off behind eyes,

then tie off at hook eye

Ray Gould

Liquid Lace Damsel

Hook = Tiemco 200R size 10

Tying thread = Tan

Tail = Fluorescent green marabou

Body = Liquid lace green tubing filled with baby oil

Eyes = Green mono

Wing stubs = Grizzly hackle fibers tied parallel to

body on each side; tie off behind eyes

NYERGES

Pattern by Gil Nyerges; modified by Ray Gould

Hook = Tiemco 200R size 8–12

Tying thread = Light olive green

Tail = Brown hackle fibers

Rib = Copper wire wound counter to palmering

Hackle = Reddish brown, palmered; clip off top and sides; must sweep back toward hook point

Body = Olive green chenille

Head = Green thread, tapered

Sparkle Back Nyerges

Hook = Tiemco 200R size 8–12

Tying thread = Light olive green

Tail = Brown hackle fibers

Shell back = Green crystal flash strands;

coat with nail polish

Rib = Copper wire counter wound

Hackle = Brown palmered; clip off top and sides

Body = Olive green chenille

Head = Green tying thread, tapered

MYLAR NYERGES

Hook = Tiemco 200R size 8–12

Tying thread = Light olive green

Tail = Brown hackle fibers

Shell back = Strip of mylar 1/8" to 3/16" Wide;

tie off at rear, then pull over top after

body, hackle and ribbing are done

Ribbing = Copper wire wound counter

Hackle = Brown palmered, clip off tops and sides

Body = Green chenille

Head = Tying thread, tapered

BLACK DRAGONFLY NYMPH

Hook = Tiemco 300R or Mustad 3665A size 8

Tying thread = Black nylon

Tail = Brown china pheasant tail feather fibers

Ribbing = Silver tinsel narrow

Body = Medium black chenille

Beard = China pheasant tail feather, fibers tied down

Shoulder = Peacock herl

Head = Black nylon tapered

Green Dragon Fly Nymph

Hook = Mustad 3665A size 6–8

Thread = Black nylon

Tail = Olive marabou

Body = Green chenille formed fat

Hackle = Brown

Eyes = Red bead pair

Thorax = Green chenille

OLIVE WILLIE

Pattern by William Serviss.

Hook = Tiemco 200R size 8–10

Tying thread = Green

Head = Red bead

Tail = Light olive marabou

Body = Green chenille

Hackle = Light olive marabou tied down as beard

Wing = Red rabbit

Head = Tie off behind bead head

BLOOD WORM

Hook = Tiemco 300R size 8

Tying thread = Black nylon

Ribbing = Copper wire wound counter

Body = Burgundy yarn

Hackle = Brown, long, 3 turns only

Head = Black tying thread, tapered

GLIMPSE BLACK LEECH

Pattern given to me by Bob Albrecht of Glimpse Lake Lodge.

Hook = Tiemco 200R size 8–10

Tying thread = Black nylon

Tail = Black hackle long as body; some fibers sticking up along top of body matuka style

Ribbing = Silver tinsel

Body = Black yarn

Hackle = Black

Head = Tapered

BYRD'S BLACK MAGIC

Invented by Jack Byrd of Edmonds.

Hook = Tiemco 300R size 8–10

Tying thread = Black nylon

Body = Medium black chenille

Wing = Black marabou 1/2" longer than bend of hook, tied on top at front

Head = Black nylon, tapered

Brown Wooly Bugger

Hook = Tiemco 200R size 8–10

Bead head = Brass

Tying thread = Tan

Tail = Brown and olive green marabou

Hackle = Brown palmered

Body = Medium brown chenille

Shoulder = Peacock herl

Head = Tie off behind bead

JANSEN

Pattern from Frank Jansen.

Hook = Tiemco 300R or Mustad 3665A size 8–10

Tying thread = Black nylon

Tail = Red hackle fibers

Ribbing = Silver tinsel

Body = Black yarn

Hackle = Black tied down as beard

Wing = Black calf's tail

Head = Black tying thread, tapered

SPRUCE FLY

Hook = Tiemco 200R size 8–10

Tying thread = Black nylon

Tail = Peacock sword feather fibers

Butt = Red yarn

Body = Peacock herl

Wing = Two badger hackles face to face,

tied on edge over top of body streamer style

Hackle = White or grizzly

Head = Small tapered black thread

Spruce Fly Nymph

Fish just under surface with slow sink tip line.

Hook = Mustad 94840 size 10

Tying thread = Black

Tail = Peacock herl fibers

Shell back = Peacock herl

Body = Light yellow yarn

Hackle = Grizzly sparse

Head = Black nylon tapered

WATER CRICKET

Hook = Tiemco 200R or Mustad 9671 size 10

Tying thread = Black nylon

Tail = Peacock herl

Ribbing = Silver tinsel

Body = Black yarn

Wing = Black hackle tips on edge over top of body

Hackle = Guinea

Head = Black nylon tapered

Royal Coachman Bucktail

Hook = Tiemco 200R or Mustad 94840 size 8–12

Tying thread = Black nylon

Tail = Red hackle fibers

Butt= Peacock herl

Body = Red yarn

Shoulder = Peacock herl

Hackle = Brown tied down

Wing = White calves tail

Head = Black tying thread, tapered

Montana Nymph

Hook = Tiemco 200R or Mustad 3665A size 8–10

Tying thread = Black nylon

Tail = Black hackle fibers

Body = Black chenille rear two-thirds, with tag

left to pull over top for wing case

Rib = Gold tinsel

Body = Yellow chenille or yarn front third

Hackle = Black tied down as beard

GILS MONSTER

A Gil Nyrerges pattern.

Hook = Tiemco 300R or Mustad 3665A size 8

Tail = None

Body = Medium black chenille

Hackle = Brown pheasant rump feather tied

spider fashion, only 2–3 turns

Head = Black tying thread, tapered

PHEASANT TAIL NYMPH

Hook = Tiemco 200R, 5212 size 10–12

Tying thread = Black nylon

Tail = Brown hackle fibers

Body = Brown hackle fibers twisted into a noodle

Shoulder = Peacock herl

Two short wings = Brown hackle fibers split to form V

Head = Black nylon thread

HARES EAR

Hook = Temco 3761 size 12

Tying thread = Tan

Bead head = Brass

Tail = Deer hair

Ribbing = Fine gold tinsel

Body = Tan dubbing

Wing case= Deer hair tied in at midpoint,

then pulled over top of dubbing

Thorax = Tan dubbing picked out to form legs

Water Boatman

Hook = Tiemco 100 or Mustad 94840 size 12

Tying thread = Black nylon

Tail = None

Wing case = Pheasant tail fibers

Body = Brown yarn

Two wings = Goose biots, one each side tied slightly down

Head = Black tying thread, tapered

CHRONOMIDS
Ice Cream Cone with Wire Rib

Hook = Tiemco 200R size 10–14

Bead head = Pearl white Spirit River 1/8"

Tying thread = Black nylon

Tail = None

Weight = Fine lead wire wound on front third

Ribbing = Copper wire or silver tinsel

Body = Black tying thread, tapered toward front

GREEN BODY CHIRONOMID

Hook = Tiemco 200R size 10–14

Bead head = Pearl white Spirit River 1/8"

Tying thread = Light olive green

Weight = Fine lead wire wrapped on front third of hook

Ribbing = Fine gold tinsel

Body = Light green yarn tapered to front

CHROMIE

Hook = Tiemco 200R or 2457 size 10–14

Bead head = Pearl white Spirit River 1/8"

Weight = Fine lead wire wrapped on front third

Tying thread = Black

Ribbing = Small red wire

Body = Silver tinsel

Thorax = Peacock herl

Gills = White antron, figure-eight wrap,

clipped short each side right behind bead head;

tie off behind gills

Ray Gould

BIG HEAD CHROMIE

Hook = Tiemco 200R or 2457 size 12

Bead head = Larger white bead

Weight = Fine lead wire front third

Rib = Red wire

Body = Silver tinsel

Shoulder = Peacock herl (no gills); theory is that it makes the fly more visible to fish

RED CHIRONOMID

Hook = Tiemco 200R size 12

Bead head = Small pearl white Spirit River

Tying Thread = Black

Weight = Fine lead wire front third

Tail = None

Body = Bright red Flashabou

Gills = White antron tied figure-eight style

behind bead head; split in two, clip short

ICE CREAM CONE WITH RED RIB

Hook = Tiemco 200R size 10–14

Bead head = Pearl white Spirit River 3/32"

Weight = Fine lead wire front third of body

Rib = Red Flashabou strip or red wire

Body = Black tying thread, tapered

MIKE'S GRAY CHIRONOMID

No photo available

Hook = tiemco 3761 size 14, two extra heavy, one extra long

Bead = 1/8" brite beads, black nickel spirit river

Tying thread = Gudebrod BCS 108 gray nylon

Rib = dark red wine colored fine wire

Body = BCS 108 gray wound to form thin body, then coated with three coats of clear fingernail polish.

Chapter 5
Fly Hook Comparison Chart

There are hundreds of different fish hooks made by a variety of manufacturers and for many different purposes. This comparison chart simplifies the choices for the fly tier by showing:

- Only trout fly fishing hooks

- Only a few of the choices (the more standard ones)

- Only three of the major manufacturers

- A minimum number of hooks to have on hand

Over the years I have favored the Tiemco hooks due to their high strength, sharpness, and small barbs. The small barbs are easily flattened to make the hook barbless. In particular favor, in my opinion, are the hooks with a straight eye because they move through the water with better movement, considering the way in which the leader is tied to the hook.

Hook Chart

Type of Use	Tiemco	Mustad	Daiichi
Dry Fly			
1x fine Turned down eye	100	94840	1100
2x long 1x fine Turned down eye	5212		1280
3x fine Turned down eye		94833	
Barbless 1x fine Turned down eye	100BL	94845	
Wet Fly/Nymphs			
1x long Turned down eye	3761		1560
2x long Turned down eye	5262	9671	1710
3x long Straight eye	200R		1270, 1770
3x long Turned down eye		9672	
1 x fine, 2xl Straight eye	2312 5212		1280
Wooly Buggers and Leeches			
3x long Straight eye	200R		1270
4x long Turned down eye		79580	
4x long Straight eye		9674	1750
6x long Straight eye	300R, heavy wire		
6x long Turned down eye		3665A	2340
Shrimp, Scuds, Chironomids	200R, 101, 100, 2457, 3761	37140, 37141, 37142, 3906	1270, X710, 1150
Steelhead	7989, 7999	9049, 36890	2421, 2441

Chapter 6

Boat Choices

The single most important item to the angler for fishing in the lakes of British Columbia for Kamloops trout is the floatation device. There are hundreds from which to choose, and there's a whole set of factors that go into each angler's decision, including portability, weight, cost, size, ability to handle a motor, color, material of construction, and durability. Samples of some of these are shown in the following photos to give the angler an idea of the broad spectrum of choices. It's important to give plenty of thought to the purchase so that the right one is selected the first time.

Boats

There is nothing quite as important to the fly fisher as a good boat. They come in all sizes and types and materials. The wood or fiberglass boats have the advantage of comfort and room and can be transported by trailer or, in some cases, by car top. The following photos show several different types:

This boat is a nine-foot plywood boat built by Maury Skeith of Seattle from a favorite pattern used by a number of friends fishing out of Cabin F at Glimpse Lake. "The Little Giant" has been adapted by William Jackson from his "Kingfisher" model, published in *Science and Mechanics*. The patterns shown on the plan were by Neely Hall. The boat is four feet wide and nine feet long, weighing one hundred pounds. It's a very stable boat and is easy to cast from when anchored. It was originally designed to be used as a sailing pram, but it makes a wonderful rowboat when the center board, mast, and sail are omitted. Nine of these boats were built after seeing the original model built by Ray Gould in 1965 (which still in use forty-four years later). Some alterations to the plan making it suitable for use with an electric motor include raising the rear seat up just below the gunnels so that a deep cycle battery can be placed beneath it, installing rubbing strips on the bottom of the boat to prevent damage to the hull, and fiberglassing all of the bottom of the boat and chines. A strong bracket on the bow is needed to hold the ten-pound anchor and pocket puller assembly.

Here's an unusual and lovely ten-foot, hand-crafted boat. Shown here with Bill Booth, it is owned by Tris Booth of Seattle and was built in Friday Harbor, Washington. The construction of the boat makes it quite light; it weighs a mere seventy pounds. The hull is made of 1/16"-thick cedar strips inside and out glued and stapled crossways to each other over a core of 3/32" marine plywood. The gunwales and frames are Alaska yellow cedar. The tread boards on the floor also appear to be yellow cedar, although it's difficult to be sure because they are painted. Note too that there are two sets of oar locks that handle the handsome spruce oars. With this setup two people can row with a third person in the stern, and the boat still balances beautifully. The boat is equipped with a substantial skeg running right to the transom and is protected with a brass plate. It is lightweight and is easy to use as a car topper. It rows easily and can handle a six-horsepower motor. The boat is beautifully finished with marine spar varnish and marine gloss white paint.

The photograph above shows Meredith Gould fishing in an eight-foot, fiberglass, lightweight boat. The estimated weight is about sixty-five pounds, making it very portable and easy to handle as a car-top boat. It was originally purchased at the Ernst Hardware store in Lynnwood, Washington

INFLATABLES

For the backpackers, here's a one-person life raft to carry on top of your pack. With oars it weighs about eight pounds. It is one of a line of "Sea Eagles" made in various sizes.

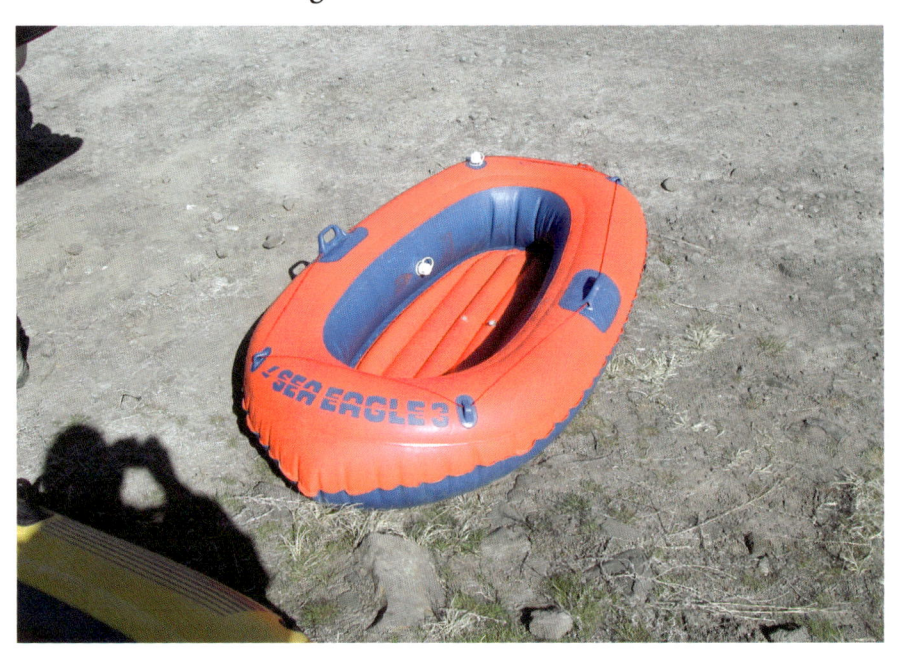

Here's another one-person raft for the backpackers. This one, owned by Hugh Clark of Seattle, was sold By REI and called the "Challenger." It has proven to be quite durable.

And don't forget the always-present "float tubes," which are available in a great many versions and used by many fly fishers.

Two boats are shown in this photo. The upper one is typical of the pontoon boats, and the lower one is a molded plastic boat. The pontoon craft is quite popular but not as roomy as wooden or fiberglass boats. Both of these are quite portable and are easy to transport.

Fold Boats

Here's a twelve-foot Porta-Bote folded up in the unassembled transport mode.

The twelve foot Porta-Bote shown here almost assembled by owner Hal Rowe is a uniquely designed folding boat. It is available in four sizes: an eight-foot model weighing forty-seven pounds, a ten-foot boat weighing fifty-nine pounds, a twelve-foot model weighing 77 pounds, and a fourteen-foot model weighing 97 pounds. These are a bit pricey but are worth the cost in portability and light weight. The boats row quite easily and also will handle an electric motor on the transom.

A boat to admire!

Dick Hankinson with his new ten-foot Acorn.

This gorgeous "klinker" boat was built by my longtime friend and fishing companion Dick Hankinson of Edmonds, Washington. It's the most beautiful piece of craftsmanship I've ever seen! It is a ten-foot "Acorn" dinghy with a forty-eight-inch beam, weighs eighty pounds, and rows like a dream. The boat was built upside down over a frame, and the final product is a one-piece hull with no internal frames. The strakes were cut from Okuma seven-millimeter marine plywood, each having five plies. The strake construction started at the keel and worked toward the gunwale, each strake overlapping the preceding strake by three quarters of an inch and glued in place using epoxy. The transom is also seven-millimeter Okuma glued to a three-quarter-inch frame for added strength. All of the wood other than the plywood is spruce, including the seats, gunwales, knees, floorboards, and keel. The boat is not fiberglassed except for the strakes on either side of the keel. Four coats of a good grade marine paint were applied, and the varnish used was also a marine grade.

The unusual curved bladed oars deserve special scrutiny. They are a modification of an eight-sided hollow spar. They are made of spruce, are 7' 4" long, and have a 1 5/8" diameter at the handle tapering down to 1 1/4" at the blade. The shafts of the oars are made up of eight staves; each stave is 11/16" wide by 5/16" thick. A notch is cut into the side of each stave using a bird's-mouth router so that the staves will fit together. All eight staves are epoxied together and are rounded off using a plane and sandpaper. The blades themselves are a work of art. They are made from two 1/4" × 6" × 20" spruce boards glued together with epoxy over a curved fame. They are then epoxied to the shafts, and a layer of fiberglass is epoxied to both sides of the blades and 10" up the shafts. This makes a very strong oar weighing only 3.4 pounds.

Ray Gould

THE SAGA OF THE *LEAKY TIKI*

As you might expect from the boat's name, *there is a story here worth telling*. It can be illustrated in pictures much better than in words, including the difficulties encountered with this boat (it leaked) and the various scientific solutions proposed.

THE PROBLEMS ILLUSTRATED

(All cartoons made for me by Leo Parr.)

"YES, I ALWAYS PULL IT UP ON THE DOCK AT NIGHT WILBER— IT SAVES SO MUCH WORK IN THE MORNING."

"I DIDN'T KNOW THE 'L' STOOD FOR 'LEAKY,' NOW HOW ABOUT CAULKING THOSE RIVETS AGAIN?"

"DID YOU EVER STOP TO THINK THAT IT MIGHT BE A SUBMARINE?"

Some Wonderful Solutions

THE ADJUSTABLE WATERLINE

THE NON-WETTED SURFACE THEORY

THE NON-DISPLACEMENT THEORY

Alas, none of the solutions quite did the job. The *Leaky Tiki* was finally incinerated in an accidental fire. What an ignominious yet fitting ending for such a famous watercraft! Author's note: Through all of this, Maury Skeith (the *Leaky Tiki*'s owner) has been, and will remain, my close friend and longtime fishing partner. He is a man for whom I have great admiration and affection.

Chapter 7

Cooking Trout

It's a real treat to taste a fresh, firm Kamloops trout. The meat is a light pink, and the taste is mild, much like that of a steelhead trout. Several ways of preparing the trout are available.

Barbequing the Kamloops Trout

One of the easiest and best is to barbeque the trout. To do this, follow these steps:

- Clean the fish, removing the head, tail, and entrails.
- Rinse thoroughly inside the body cavity and outside as well.
- Place the fish on a sheet of aluminum foil large enough to wrap the fish completely.
- Inside the body cavity place the following:
- Thin slices of onion
- Thin slices of lemon
- Thin slices of garlic
- Wrap the fish up in the aluminum foil.
- Place the trout in a preheated barbeque and cook at 350 degrees Fahrenheit for 25-30 minutes, depending on the size of the trout.
- Put the trout on a cutting board or in a pan (to catch the juices) and open up the foil.
- If the fish is adequately cooked, the skin of the fish will come off when the foil is peeled back from the top. Then take a spatula and run it down along the backbone from front to back, removing the top fillet of the trout.
- Grasp the backbone at the front and lift it out as a unit. Almost all the bones will be removed in one piece.
- Serve the trout with salt, pepper, and barbeque sauce.

SMOKING KAMLOOPS TROUT

Another favorite of many folks is smoking the trout. Here's a good recipe for the salt mix to put on a trout before smoking:

- 1 cup brown sugar
- 1 cup salt
- 1 tsp ground garlic (minced)
- 1 Tbsp onion powder
- 3/4 tsp white pepper
- 1 tsp basil
- 1 tsp Italian herb mix
- 3/4 tsp dill seed (whole)

Mix these together thoroughly in a mixing bowl and place in a mason jar with a perforated lid. Store in a cool place.

DIRECTIONS

- Cut the fish into two fillets.
- Before smoking, smear the mix on the flesh side of the trout and some on the exterior, too.
- Use a Little Chief Smoker or a Big Chief Smoker by Luhr Jensen (110 volt). Place alder or apple wood chips in the pan provided, filling it evenly. Preheat the smoker before putting in the fish or the wood chips.
- Remove the rack from the smoker and fill it with trout, placing the largest pieces on the bottom, flesh side up (skin side down).
- Smoke for 6–8 hours, refilling the wood chip pan about once per hour.
- Remove the rack, remove the trout using a spatula, and wrap the fish in newspaper covered with aluminum foil. Store in the refrigerator.

This provides a real treat and makes a wonderful hors d'oeuvre.

TROUT PÂTÉ (SOURCE: WIL WATSON)

Another treat for serving the trout is to make it into a pâté. This can be served on crackers prior to a meal. Here's the information as to how to make the pâté.

Ingredients

- 1 fifteen-inch smoked trout
- 1/3 carton cream cheese
- 1/3 carton plain yogurt
- 1 tsp liquid smoke
- 1 tsp Tabasco
- 1 tbsp parsley flakes
- 2 tbsp olive oil

Directions

- Fine grind the trout.
- Add seasonings and stir.
- Stir in the cheese and yogurt (soften them in a microwave first).
- Keep in sealed containers in the refrigerator.
- Serve on crackers.

Chapter 8

Discovering Nature

ONE OF THE AMAZING THINGS that happens to many fly fishers is that they discover the beauty of nature in the flowers and birds of British Columbia. The area near fly fishing lakes is rife with flora and fauna. Sooner or later many will get out their cameras and reference books to identify what they see in order to share them with others.

The purpose of this chapter is to share with the reader what might be encountered, with the hope that he or she will gain an appreciation of nature and will understand why the public must strive to preserve it for future generations.

The following photographs show some of the flowers native to the area where Kamloops trout are found.

Red Columbine

148

Columbine in many colors can be found growing wild.

Roses such as this are abundant along the roadsides in British Columbia.

Particularly abundant in British Columbia are fields of lupine in blue and white.

Ray Gould

A solitary arnica was found near Calling Lake.

Aster

Paintbrush

Tiger Lily or Columbia Lily

Ray Gould

Wildflowers forever (lupine)

What's this Pinto doing in my wildflowers?

The Aspens fall colors

This very unusual magenta-colored lupine was given to me in seed form by Ruth Ann Pennell and Dave Doneux of Seattle, Washington. Lupines are hard to start from seeds (at least for me), and this is the only one that sprouted and came up after planting about fifty seeds. Nonetheless, I'll try again; they are such a lovely plant.

Ray Gould

The Birds of British Columbia

(All bird photos by Wil Watson)

British Columbia is a bird watcher's paradise. There are a tremendous number of species, and only a sampling is shown in the following photographs. The birds of British Columbia are a hungry bunch. All one has to do to attract all kinds of them is to hang up a bird feeder and a suet feeder. Each will attract different kinds of birds. And don't forget a hummingbird feeder, too, because there are many who will visit each day.

The Evening Grosbeak comes north in the early spring and will usually stay for two to three weeks.

This Hairy Woodpecker loves the suet feeder right outside my cabin porch.

Canada Geese with young ones are becoming more and more common.

Clark's Nutcracker also prefers suet.

Ray Gould

This Yellow-headed Blackbird is always the "king of the roost."

The always present Mallard, this one a drake.

Barrow's Goldeneye

Among the many other commonly seen birds in British Columbia are these: loons, downy woodpeckers, pileated woodpeckers, flickers, ospreys, bald eagles, red-tailed hawks, barn swallows, red-breasted nuthatches, white breasted nuthatches, grebes, blue herons, redwing blackbirds, brewers blackbirds, and bufflehead ducks. A capable photographer with a good camera can have a great deal of fun snapping photos of all of these birds!

Mushrooms

For those who are expert in the study and recognition of fungi (mycologists), there are plenty of wild mushrooms to be found in the forests of British Columbia. Among the more commonly found and highly prized edible mushrooms are the following:

- The morel (*Morchella eschlenta*), found in the springtime. This mushroom is easily recognized by its distinctive shape and color.

- The golden chanterelle (*Cantharellus Cibarius*), found in July.

- The King Bolete (*Boletus Edulis*), also known as porcini.

- The shaggy mane (*Coprinus Comatus*), an inky cap found in the fall season.

A special note to would-be mushroom pickers: It has been well put by this quote from Klingensmith: "There are old mushroom hunters and bold mushroom hunters but no old, bold mushroom hunters." *Be extremely careful in picking mushrooms.* There are many species that can kill you or make you very ill. You must be absolutely sure the mushroom you are picking is edible.

Chapter 9

Recommendations: Choosing the Right Place

Fly fishers have a number of favorite ways to pursue the wily Kamloops trout. Some prefer to seek remoteness and privacy and thus go backpacking into the lakes far off the beaten path; it's a great way to get close to nature. This appeals to the younger anglers and those who are in good shape and are not held back by the infirmities of old age. Other anglers prefer to visit campsites and pitch their tents, campers, or small trailers to enjoy the outdoors. This is certainly an economical way to find good fishing, but on occasion it can be crowded and noisy. Then there are those who wish to take an RV, motor home, or trailer on their fishing adventure.

Selecting the best lake to visit is no small task, but it is an important one. One of the first considerations is to determine whether the lake has the type of facilities desired for the particular trip. For example, if you are towing a big trailer or driving an RV, then it's necessary to find a spot that can be accessed, has space, and perhaps has hook-ups.

Usually fishing in a lake where there are big fish to be caught is a primary factor. For this reason study the triploid planting data found elsewhere in this book will guide you to those places. Another way of deciding is to review the fish density document found in this chapter. A third consideration is how far away the lake is from home and whether time is available to get there and back.

Putting all this together, I have the following recommendations.

- For a day trip or camping trip, visit **Marquart** and **Lundbom Lakes.** These two lakes, close to Merritt, are right together and can be fished on the same trip. Both lakes are stocked with triploids and are easy to get to. Marquart and Lundbom are very popular and well utilized, so it's best to select a weekday and avoid holidays.

- For a lodge stay where rooms, meals, and boats are provided and the angler wishes to be pampered a bit, try **Minnie** and **Stoney Lakes** on the Douglas Lake Ranch. Those two lakes are also right together and can be fished on the same trip. A nice lodge is provided at Stoney Lake. Another highly recommended place in this category is the **Corbett Lake County Inn** about twelve miles out of Merritt. Cabins, meals, and boats are offered. Note that owner Peter McVey is a cordon bleu chef. This lake is privately owned and operated and is well stocked with huge fish.

- When pulling a house trailer or driving an RV, consider going to **Dragon Lake**. It's quite a bit farther north but worth the trip because it's famous for turning out very large Kamloops trout. Dragon Lake is located right next to the city of Quesnel, which is some 480 miles from Seattle. Note too that besides RV hookups, camping facilities are available. As an unique feature they have house trailers parked, hooked up, and ready for rental. Another good spot in this category is **Tunkwa Lake,** north of the town of Logan Lake. It is strongly stocked, including triploids, and is widely known for its terrific chironomid hatches. Tunkwa Lake provides camping, trailering, or RVs. Study the fish density chart in the chapter "To Get an Edge." It shows that the number of fish stocked per acre is quite high and should result in some great fishing.

- For the fly fisher who wishes a more remote camping spot and is not necessarily after lunker trout, consider **Fawn Lake** or **Plateau Lake**. It's best to have a truck or SUV, preferably with four-wheel drive, to attempt the visit to Plateau Lake. See the chapter "Twenty-six of the Best Lakes in British Columbia" for information as to how to get to these two lakes.

- For all around good fishing, try **Roche Lake** south of the city of Kamloops. It is well stocked, although it is very popular with local fly fishers and is often crowded.

- Backpackers have a special treat in store for them if they make the trek into **Myrtle Lake** in Wells Gray Provincial Park. Canoes can be rented in Blue River, and the portage is only one and a quarter miles using a two-wheeled dolly. In the same park is the **Stevens Lakes** chain. I have been there eleven times and have found terrific fishing, but the trek is arduous. Remember, you must take everything you need with you, including a small raft. Count on your pack weighing sixty to sixty-five pounds for a four- to five-day trip. Plan to go with others as a safety precaution and have a compass and map with you.

Some final thoughts:

1. Remember to have your passport with you if coming from or going to the United States.

2. If possible, avoid traveling on Friday or Sunday, because the border crossings are quite busy.

3. Plan your trip well in advance, especially if a reservation is needed.

A LIST OF ESPECIALLY WORTHY LAKES TO VISIT IN BRITISH COLUMBIA.

For comparison, the average fish density of the twenty-six best lakes is sixty fish per acre.

1. **Marquart:** 57 acres; about 1/2 of stock is triploids each year for the last 5 years (2005–2009); fish density 149 fish/acre; near Merritt.

2. **Lundbom:** 114 acres; 6,000 triploids in 2007; 79 fish/acre; near Merritt, easy access.

3. **Dragon:** 556 acres, 10,000 Triploids each year last 5 years, 45 fish/acre, near Quesnel. Known for very large fish.

4. **Roche:** 326 acres, heavy plant each year for the last 5 years, including triploids; 69 fish/acre; near Kamloops.

5. **Dugan:** 238 acres; 147 fish/acre in 2009, with 57% rainbow triploids; near Williams Lake.

6. **Forest:** 240 acres; 20,000 triploids each year for the last 8 years (2001- 2009), 83 fish/acre; near Williams Lake.

7. **Jewel:** 184 acres; triploids planted 2006–2009; 109 Fish /acre; near Greenwood. All-time biggest rainbow came from this lake.

8. **Minnie (300 acres) and Stoney (150 acres):** both lakes planted with 25,000 rainbows in 2006, they are close to each other and part of the Douglas Lake Ranch. Consistently produce big fish.

9. **Crystal:** 135 acres; triploids planted 2006–2009; 259 fish/acre; 3 miles south of Bridge Lake.

10. **Fawn:** 79 acres; highest fish/acre at 189; on the Bridge Lake road; good accommodations.

Chapter 10

When All Else Fails

Don't get discouraged when fishing is slow and you just can't seem to connect with the trout. Over the years I have learned there are several sure-fire ways to attract the fish. These inveterate systems can be sworn to by many a seasoned fly fisher. Try one of these proven ways.

- Put your fly rod down and let the fly just drift along. Then begin eating a sandwich and drinking a cup of hot coffee. As soon as you do, a vicious strike will occur. Now try to eat the soggy sandwich dropped in the bottom of the boat during all the excitement and pour yourself another cup of coffee!

- Make a perfect cast, then look up at the contrail of a passing jet airliner. You'll probably have a broken leader when the smashing strike comes so unexpectedly!

- Sooner or later, as you're mooching your fly along a particularly good shoal, you'll find the need to relieve yourself. This can really be disastrous but quite memorable! Some find it difficult to plan ahead for this event.

- If you like to mooch the fly by rowing slowly, try turning a relatively sharp corner while looking over your shoulder to see where you're going. That's precisely when the fish hits and the rod goes overboard. (I've personally been there and done that!)

- After an hour or two of casting in your favorite spot with no luck, the fish finally start rising. Somehow in all the excitement, that's when you get the world's biggest fly line tangle in the bottom of the boat. By the time you get straightened out and a new fly and leader tied on, the rise is over!

- Try fishing "last week"; that's when it was really good! A past acquaintance by the name of Mac McLaughlin always responded to that by saying, "Hell, I was here last week, and it wasn't any good then either."

- Maybe I've been chasing the wrong kind of rainbow!

A fitting way to end this book is with a story so improbable that almost no one will believe it—yet this actually happened to me, and I'll swear on a stack of Bibles it's true.

The event took place on a lovely June afternoon at Glimpse Lake several years ago. I left the dock in my nine-foot boat and used my electric motor to travel across the lake to one of my favorite spots, a shoal where the water was about six feet deep. I dropped the anchor and rigged up my favorite Nyerges Nymph fly with a sink tip fly line on one of my bamboo rods. There was only one other angler fishing nearby, so I had plenty of room. After a few casts there was a smashing strike and a terrific screaming of the reel as a large Kamloops trout ripped off line and jumped high in the air. I stripped in line furiously to catch up with the fish, and then off he'd go, time and again, with another run and leap showing his silvery sides. Then to my great dismay, it was suddenly over. The leader had broken right where the fly had been tied on. I sat down muttering to myself with my knees still shaking and tied on another Nyerges Nymph. I stood up, preparing to cast in the same area as before.

Now here's the unbelievable event: At the exact time I made this cast, a beautiful and large trout jumped up high in the air some sixty feet away—right where I had cast just as my line straightened out above the water. I saw the leader glint in the sun as it passed over the back of the fish. It was pure reflex that caused me to rear back on the fly line, and sure enough I snagged the fish while it was in midair. Now the battle really began because it was a big fish that had leverage against me because it was foul hooked. It must have taken fifteen minutes to finally net that fish. There in the corner of his mouth was my other Nyerges Nymph. It was the same fish that had broken off minutes before. It weighed some three to four pounds; what a treasure! Yes, it is true, honest!

Map Resources

Department of Energy, Mines, Resources, map 92 I/1, Merritt
Department of Energy, Mines, Resources, map 93 C, Anaheim Lake
Department of Energy, Mines, Resources, map 92 I, Ashcroft
Department of Energy, Mines, Resources, map 92 I/14, Cache Creek
Department of Energy, Mines, Resources, map 92 P/14, Lac La Hache
Department of Energy, Mines, Resources, map 92 I/11, Ashcroft
Department of Energy, Mines, Resources, map 92 P, Bonaparte Lake
Department of Energy, Mines, Resources, map 93 C/6, Anaheim Lake
Department of Energy, Mines, Resources, map 92 P/15, Canim Lake
Department of Energy, Mines, Resources, map 93 C/11, Christensen Creek
Department of Energy, Mines, Resources, map 92 I/10, Cherry Creek
Federal Publications, map 092 I/1, Merritt
Federal Publications, map 092 I/14, Heffley Creek
Federal Publications, map 092 I/9, Kamloops
Federal Publications, map 092 I/2, Merritt
Federal Publications, map 092 I/8, Stump Lake
Federal Publications, map 92 I/7, Mamit lake
Federal Publications, map 92 I/6, Spences Bridge
Backroad Mapbooks, BCTOPO map TOBC21
Backroad Mapbooks, BCTOPO map TOBC14
Backroad Mapbooks, BCTOPO map TOBC20
Backroad Mapbooks, BCTOPO map TOBC19
The Kamloops & District Fish and Game & Game Association, Fishing and Hunting Map, Centennial Edition.

BIBLIOGRAPHY

Brooks, Charles, *Nymph Fishing for Larger Trout*, Winchester Press, 1976.

Raymond, Steve, *The Estuary Flyfisher*, Frank Amato Publications, 1996.

Fly Pattern Encyclopedia Federation of Fly Fishers, Frank Amato Publications, 2000.

Rickards, Denny, *Tying Stillwater Patterns for Trophy Trout*, Stillwater Productions, 2002.

Raymond, Steve, *Kamloops an Anglers Study of the Kamloops Trout*, Frank Amato Publications, 1994.

Haig-Brown, Roderick, *A Primer of Fly Fishing*, William Morrow Inc, 1964.

Raymond, Steve, *The Year of the Angler*, Winchester Press, 1983.

Lawson, Mike and LaFontaine, *Fly Fishing the Henry's Fork*, Greycliff Publishing, 2000.

Bradner, Enos, *Northwest Angling*, Binford and Mort Publishing Co., 1950.

Inland Empire Fly Fishing Club, *Flies of the Northwest*, Frank Amato Publications, 1998.

Raymond, Steve, *Blue Upright*, Lyons Press, 2004.

Raymond, Steve, *Rivers of the Heart*, Lyons Press, 1998.

A.J. Campbell, *Fly Fishing Tackle*, Lyons and Burford, 1997.

Richardson, Lee, *Lee Richardson's BC*, Champoeg Press, 1978.

Brooks, Wade, *Fly Fishing and the Meaning of Life*, Voyageur Press, 2006.

Rowley, Phillip, *Fly Patterns for Stillwater*, Frank Amato Publications, 2000.

Kaufman, Randall, *Fly Tyer's Nymph Manual*, Western Fisherman's Press, 1986.

Sibley, David, *The Sibley Guide to Birds*, Alfred Knopf, 2000.

The Audubon Society, *Field Guide to North American Birds*, Alfred Knopf, 1971.

Hellekson, Terry, *Popular Fly Patterns*, Peregrine Smith, 1976.

Chartrand, Claude, *The Art of Fly Tying*, Firefly Books Inc., 1972.

Flick, Art, *Master Fly Tying Guide*, Crown Publishers Inc., 1972.

Bruhn, Karl, *Lake Fishing*, Frank Amato Publications, 1992.

Hill, Les and Graham Marshall, *Stalking Trout*, SeTo Publishing, 1985.

Traver, Robert, *Trout Madness*, St. Martin's Press, 1960.

Gerlach, Rex, *Creative Fly Tying and Fly Fishing*, Stoeger Publishing Co., 1974.

Lingren, Aurther, *Fly Patterns of British Columbia*, Frank Amato Publications, 1996.

Kling, Paul, *The Basic Manual of Fly-Tying*, Sterling Publishing Co., 1979.